T0155306

ADVANCE PRAISE

Life Lines: Re-Writing Lives from Inside Out

In the pages of "Life Lines," these women are not inmates, they are writers. Though so often describing how the system – and sometimes one's own regrets – can reduce a whole human to "a chocolate drop so small/not even a butterfly can taste it," readers will surely experience the inverse: expansive, full-bodied, unique, necessary voices. Women who, as Whitman said, contain multitudes. This collection is a lyrical *movement*, built on the tenants of art, education and advocacy. The women in "Life Lines" begin to shape a possible future – one that embraces restorative practices over our failing system of punishment. They restore my hope.

> Caits Meissner, Director, Prison and Justice Writing Program, PEN America, NY

Here is another remarkable book from *writinginsideVT*. It is overflowing with the creativity and voices of the most invisible women in our society: women in prison. Despite the sadness, fear, pain, and loss that they convey, their written words are a testament to the resilience of women's spirit.

> Stephanie S. Covington, Ph.D., Co-director, Center for Gender and Justice, La Jolla, CA

Forty-three years in the justice system, as prosecutor, defense attorney and judge, have taught me that events beyond their control incarcerate women: childhood neglect; sexual, physical and emotional abuse; and their inevitable sequelae – substance abuse and mental health issues. Unaddressed, the feelings from these traumatic events will only fester, cause more pain, then recidivism. Art and writing have repeatedly proven to be a powerful and curative outlet for these feelings. Writing gives them voice when no one speaks for them; empowers them to cast away the pain, anger and emotional restraints; and allows us to know their feelings inside, getting out, and outside. Their expression, and our acceptance of it, give life to the 'restoration' in restorative justice. Read these poems and understand the pain, fear and anger that is at their heart.

Hon. Joseph H. Field, Active Retired Judge, Maine District Court

The criminal justice system spends a great deal of time trying to establish the 'otherness' of people. Yet, every person has a story to tell. These writings show our common humanity and the need to hear all voices.

Robert L. Sand, Director, Center for Justice Reform, VT Law School; former Windsor County State's Attorney

"LIFE LINES: Re-Writing Lives from Inside Out" is a must-read for those interested in the psychological dynamics of women's incarceration and reentry, as seen from the inside out. Fruit of a ten-year writing program *writinginsideVT* has held in Vermont's only prison for women, these poems beautifully capture the experience of incarcerated women trying to make sense of their past choices and daring to make new ones. Difficult, often brutally honest, funny, remorseful, grief-stricken, defiant, self-accusing and self-affirming, these poems explore the devastating hold of their addictions, the cycling nature of their incarceration, and the very real costs not only to themselves but to their families and other victims. The editors, Bianca Viñas, Sarah W. Bartlett, and Kassie Tibbott, have organized the book effectively around the themes of voice, loss, creativity, new patterns and hope, themes beautifully illustrated by Meg Reynolds.

Heather Tosteson, Ph.D. Publisher, Wising Up Press, GA; Co-Director, *The Lasting Weight of Felony Listening Project*

Expression and voice are so important to hear from those incarcerated in our Vermont prisons. This book celebrates the vital minds and hearts of those we often do not hear.

Bess O'Brien, director of award-winning documentaries "Coming Home" (about re-entry from prison) and "The Hungry Heart" (about addiction recovery), Kingdom County Productions, VT

LIFE LINES

LIFE LINES

RE-WRITING LIVES
FROM INSIDE OUT

BIANCA VIÑAS, SARAH W. BARTLETT
& KASSIE TIBBOTT, EDITORS
MEG REYNOLDS, ILLUSTRATOR

Printed in the United States

10 9 8 7 6 5 4 3 2 1

Green Writers Press is a Vermont-based publisher whose mission is to spread a message of hope and renewal through the words and images we publish. Throughout we will adhere to our commitment to preserving and protecting the natural resources of the earth. To that end, a percentage of our proceeds will be donated to environmental activist groups and South Burlington Community Justice Center. Green Writers Press gratefully acknowledges support from individual donors, friends, and readers to help support the environment and our publishing initiative.

Giving Voice to Writers & Artists Who Will Make the World a Better Place
Green Writers Press | Brattleboro, Vermont
www.greenwriterspress.com

ISBN: 978-1-9505841-7-8

This publication is funded in part by grants from *BCA Community Fund* and the *Serena Foundation*.

Book and Cover Design: Sarah W. Bartlett
Cover Image: Meg Reynolds

Printed on recycled paper by Bookmobile.
Based in Minneapolis, Minnesota, Bookmobile began as a design and typesetting production house in 1982 and started offering print services in 1996. Bookmobile is run on 100% wind- and solar-powered clean energy.

*"We are our stories,
stories that can be both prison and the crowbar
to break open the door of that prison."*
— Rebecca Solnit

*"I am more than I ever thought I could be —
the full story of renewal and growth.
If I don't take the risk to change,
everything I've learned will go to waste."*
— *wiVT* participant

ACKNOWLEDGEMENTS

Cover image first appeared in a different form as "Cat's Cradle," Meg Reynolds, *Utterance: A Journal*, 2 Oct. 2018 www.utterancejournal.com/three-pieces-meg-reynolds/ Meg's other illustrations appear in print for the first time here.

*   *   *

Many of the women whose work appears in the following pages are still incarcerated. Their written permission to use their work — as with those already released — identifies them as they requested. Per Department of Corrections (DOC) requirements, specific names, places and other identifiers have been removed from the work of those still under DOC supervision. No other editing has occurred.

Each writing is in response to a prompt, which can often be a poem or quotation. Where a specific line has been used as the title of the piece, its source is noted here in the order in which it appears in the following pages:

"Action is a great restorer and builder of confidence. Inaction is not only the result, but the cause of fear." - Normal Vincent Peale, "The Power of Positive Thinking," Touchstone, 2003

"When patterns are broken, new worlds emerge." — Tuli Kupferberg

"Hope is better than fear, optimism better than despair." — Jack Layton

"Let things happen rather than make them happen." — Gerald Jampolsky

LIFE LINES

"You're always with yourself, so you might as well enjoy the company." – Diane Von Furstenberg

"I walked in a summer twilight / looking for my daughter ..." from 'The Pomegranate' by Eavan Boland, "In a Time of Violence," W. W. Norton & Company, Inc., 1994.

"... I know I need to belong to myself." – Sue Monk Kidd, "The Mermaid Chair," Viking Press, 2005.

"Something has tried to kill me / and has failed." – from 'won't you celebrate with me' by lucille clifton, "Book of Light," Copper Canyon Press, 1993.

"I am an instrument in the shape / of a woman," from 'Planetarium' by Adrienne Rich, "The Fact of a Doorframe: Selected Poems 1950-2001," W. W. Norton and Company Inc., 2002.

*　　*　　*

The final poem, 'Am I This Mystery Woman?,' is an example of our routine practice of creating a 'found poem' using lines from each woman's writing the previous session, then closing the current group with that poem. In essence, this tapestry of participants' individual voices rises to the communal level of meaning and experience. The final lines often echo a positive message found in the writings. In this case,

> *"All I really see is a strong woman*
> *who believes in who she is now."*

Editorial Note

Each week for the past ten years, Vermont's sole women's prison has opened its doors to a pair of volunteers from *writinginsideVT*. On Thursday evenings, a dozen or more inmates could be found circled up at the table with our team, prepared to honor their truths and let their words spill unedited from their hearts and pens. The writings, which remain in this raw form on the following pages, cry pain, beg for help, whisper despair, suggest remorse, seek hope, and demand second chances. Such release of layered emotions – along with the opportunity to be validated and encouraged to reflect – has, in the words of many *writinginsideVT* writers, "provided a lifeline" through their incarceration.

*"I want to feel what I feel, even if it's not happiness.
I'm done hiding behind the mask."* - *wiVT* participant

WHISPER TO VOICE

LOSS AND LONGING

CREATIVITY WITHIN

WHEN PATTERNS ARE BROKEN

AND STILL WE HOPE

WHISPER TO VOICE

"Action is a great restorer and builder of confidence. Inaction is not only the result, but the cause of fear." - Normal Vincent Peale
    Sarah

I have stood in the cold wind of morning. Watched my face reflected back at me through placid river water. Wondering why. What change I could possibly facilitate. How my hands could leave ripples in the world, altering it just enough to leave an imprint, however faint. I fear I may be buried in the mud and fossilized before my impression is discovered.

I know that fear is a driving force behind many of my actions. I would rather confidence bridge the gap. Though it seems we don't have that in surplus. If we could feed the hungry fear, and power the world with inaction, we would want for nothing. Though, I would rather stand firm knowing that my choice could spark a revolution.

One voice, one phrase, a sentence even can change history. I want love, but I fight against it. Rather, I would bury it down and let it burn inside me, curbing the fear, and keeping it company. If it is worth fighting for, if it truly means enough, the world stops turning just for you. Long enough that you can place your hand in the mold. What are we, if not different, unique? People gave their lives – for freedom, for the right to be a human being. They marched until their feet bled and sang until their throats ran dry. Because they believed in the rightness of their cause. I too would walk until my legs gave way and I would crawl. I believe in everything those people have done. They set fire to my heart ...

Where has that passion gone, the idea of fighting for what is right, what we believe in? Does it seem radical to take a stand against injustice or aggression? I find nothing riveting or consequential in the daily monotony of my life here. Does that mean no one else feels anything anymore? If they love as I do. If they fear it. Are we all just hiding from the world with our eyes closed? When it's discussed, I hope my name ignites passion, and leaves a taste of understanding.

VIEW FROM THE CONCRETE WORLD
*wi*VT participant

With a single step, and one wrong choice, now I live in a concrete world, on an invisible rollercoaster that is in a house of horror. You must give up control. Make no plans, don't get too close. It's too cold, it's too hot, never comfortable. Keep moving. Don't cry. Everyone will ask you why. Don't hang pictures on the wall. They will only get ripped when you have to move them again, pushed this way and that. My body is getting weak. My heart wants to bleed. I have been abused again. The outside world never sees. I scream inside wanting others to see the things that they to do me. There is no word, just pain, tears, put downs, fake concern. You hold out your hand but I don't dare reach. Will you pull it away before I get there or will someone tell you she is not good enough or will the people of the wall cut it off?

Always remember - you are wrong, you are a criminal and you have no voice.

MY FIVE SENSES
wiVT participant

As I sit here, I hear the slamming of doors. Oh, how I hate that sound, but you get accustomed to it. As I sit here, I smell the jolly ranchers and mints. Thank God that's what I smell. As I sit here, I can taste the mint in my mouth - should I offer one to my neighbor?

As I sit here, I imagine how I want to reach out and touch someone and just to give a friend a hug, to let them know that they are not alone. As I sit here, I sit here in darkness, but I've got to remember that I'm also not alone...

LUDICROUS
Cindy

I begin my days
at the 8 am current events class.
I have continued this ritual
for almost two years now.
Today the teacher was sharing
a story from his past.
He was going overseas and when his plane landed,
he was very sick, his throat raw, head pounding.
He sought out the pharmacy.
What he knew would help,
 "Sudafed," could not be bought.
He was told by the pharmacist
he needed to put a slip in, go see a doctor,
then return in five days.
He thought this ludicrous
but it was not a joke. It seems "Sudafed"
was used to make a drug by those cooking Meth.
It sounds just like what we have to go
through here in prison.
If you have a headache, migraine, sore throat
or feel nauseous,
you go to Medical; or I should say
you TRY to go to Medical,
only to be stopped and told
you have to put in a slip.
So, you suffer through your illness
with no help or compassion from anyone.

If you are lucky, you might get a Tylenol
or be told you have to buy that on commissary.
Commissary can be ordered only once a week.
A package of two pills cost almost $0.30.
We are allowed to purchase five packs only.
Sounds ludicrous, right?
But true.
Today, I am on day three of a migraine.
I submitted so many slips
even before those three excruciating days
because my head began aching
a few days before it turned
into a migraine.
So, things are the same for us today
as my teacher experienced
many years ago.
Just think, if you have a headache
you simply take a couple of pills
that are at your fingertips.
You don't wait five days or have to
put in a slip to get help.
Also, you probably paid $3.00
for a bottle of 100.
Now figure out how much that
would cost us to buy 100.

IN THIS PLACE
M. Ga

In this place, I've been robbed of my identity. I have been gas-lighted, made to believe I am insignificant or unworthy. You talk about abusive relationships. I'd rather have one abuser than several. Everywhere you turn - *don't do this, don't do that* ... Living life walking on eggshells. Eventually you grow accustomed. It becomes a natural part of life. At which point you have lost your soul. You no longer know how to depict your interests or to express your own feelings. Every possible variation of self-expression has been stripped from you. You are told, *behave this way or else* ... The consequences for standing up for what you believe in are severe. Locked in a room with nothing but metal for days on end. Left to your own devices. The system is cruel and brutal. It's true I have a hard time deciding anything for myself because I'm waiting for a dictator to demean, belittle and eventually ruin me. Rob you of your very essence, what you were raised on. Your moral and value systems destroyed. Just another passerby fallen victim to corruption.

HOW TO SAVE THE WORLD
FROM THE HEROIN EPIDEMIC
E.N.

Take a small time (or big time) dealer, someone who sells here and there to support their own habit. Tell them that one of the bags they just sold killed one of their close friends or family members and they are now going to jail for manslaughter, 2 ½ - 20 years. Bring them straight to jail where they will detox cold turkey with nothing but Tylenol and antidiarrheal meds and sleep on a half inch of foam on top of a metal slab; or attempt to sleep anyway because they won't get more than an hour for the first thirty days. Take them off all their legitimate prescriptions, antidepressants, antipsychotics, sleep meds, pain meds, shit, even their antacids; and tell them that every illness, pain, disease, and dysfunction they have ever been diagnosed with isn't real and that they are just an addict. Put them in with a bunch of sadistic bitches who will call them a killer and say they did it on purpose and that they didn't love or care about the person who died…now leave that person there to marinate for three months before offering a chance on the outside where they can choose to either cook their ass or…

I AM SMART

wiVT participant

I am smart
      but you say I'm not
I am smart
      then you say I am a joke
I am smart
      you laugh in my face and say, *please, don't lie to yourself*
I am smart
      you just laugh
I am smart
      but you tell me to stop dreaming
I am smart
      you still pick on me
I am smart
      you tell me to shut up
I am smart
      then you ask me *to who, again?* and say I'm nothing but a joke
I still reply I am smart

I am smart

I am smart

IN THIS PLACE I LIVE IN
wiVT participant

In this place I live in,
     there are drug dealers, murderers and abusers.
In this place I live in,
     there are liars, haters and people that are scared.
In this place I live in,
     we look out one window from every room. It is very cold; but
so sunny.
In this place I live in,
     it seems like it will never end
In this place I live in,
     when will I ever go home?
In this place I live in,
     things are unknown.
In this place I live in,
     I am not alone.

PORK CHOP TRAIN

Dani

What have I become?
a number
149877
What have I become?
an animal
chow, come and get it.
What have I become?
personality-less
me.

I once was a girl
but I was scared to go to bed.
I once was a teen
but I got scared about the epidural.
I once was a mom
but I got scared they'd feel my pain.
I once was a carpenter
but I got scared of success.
I once was a booster
but I got scared of getting caught.
I once was a dealer
but I got suspicious of everything.
I once was an active addict
but I got scared of death.

I once wasn't scared of anything
but I gotta grow up.
What have I become
besides an inmate?
I try to answer that question.
I try to remember who I was
before the pain and before the drugs.
What have I become?
Nothing more than me -
shitty tattoos, some inward and surface
scars. Some days I'm amazing
and others, I have a shitty attitude.
What have I become?
Me,

same me as ever.
What did I become?
Everything I can be.

And I keep going. Because
if there's one thing I do
it is continue.

HOPE
Melissa

Hope has no goddamned wings. Perhaps she had them once, a shining Christmas angel full-feathered. Now she staggers, wet cobblestones dripping bloody stumps, stray feathers mutilated with her blood. She weeps and wails, sorry for herself, sorry for me. Hope has no goddamned wings. She doesn't wear a sparkling samite sheath. She wears tattered rags, too worn and stained to be black, too mottled to be gray. Her muddy petticoat bares torn lace, my Freudian slip showing. Hope has no goddamned wings. Her feet bleed with every halting step, the mean and bitter earth cutting and snatching, tearing and rending tender, once-pristine feet. Hope has no goddamned wings. She was shot down long ago, if she ever flew at all on wings made of the dreams of fools. Hope has no goddamned wings. I've never seen her face shining with holy light, only wet with sweat and tears, folded like a Japanese fan with effort. Hope has no goddamned wings. She doesn't sing a victory tune. She compels me on with a fucking dirge - mine - if I don't work harder, faster, longer, better ... mine, if I'm lucky. Hope has no goddamned wings.

MEDITATION
wiVT participant

I'm scared to meditate because then I'm forced to be grounded, here in prison where we aren't human. The smell...UGH. The dreaded smell of House 2 is all I can think of. The unit I live in, it constantly stinks. The windows don't open, the women don't shower, and the ones that do brush their remaining teeth clearly aren't doing it proper.

The drain on the floor in the shower room, center of the floor, oh how it smells like a rotting carcass. Actually, roadkill would smell better. At least it's still fresh. The only thing fresh about House 2 is the mess. It's been all day with no paper towels and now we're running out of tissue too. Oh, whatever are we to do. Those of us who do bathe and brush are tired of having to live as such. Our unit cleaner is a grumpy little dwarf who doesn't clean the showers and if you complain, she'll want you to help out, yet she's the one getting paid the two dollars. All hell's gonna break loose tonight if I wake up in the middle of the night and have to drip dry.

LIVING ON THE INSIDE
Cindy

Living on the inside,
being controlled in every direction,
ordered around every corner,
rules barked at us, as if we are nothing.

Living on the inside
a broken existence, ready to snap,
when our tiny being is pushed
to the limit of no return.

Living on the inside,
a maze with no way out,
rooms with looming odors,
dingy walls, dirty windows, no air.

Living on the inside--
if you haven't experienced it,
you really don't have a clue.
This unbelievable state of condition
grows within us like a cancer diagnosis.

We will stumble many times,
feel tossed like a ping-pong ball.
Our beings deteriorate. We feel small.
That's the truth of living on the inside.

MAXED OUT AND HOMELESS
wiVT participant

When I came to jail, I was homeless for a long time, so I sat on lack of residence for seven months, five months past my first minimum date. I went to Dismas House, that didn't work out. Came back in November, then sat past my minimum date again for five months. Then I got out to my brother's house, did good for a while, but I had no contact with my wife, so I took off on escape for six weeks. I do not regret that at all. That was the only time this year I had spent with her before she died.

Then I came back to jail until August. I told my P.O. it wouldn't work. Lo and behold, six days later I was in jail yet again.

Now I've sat here for three months, but this time I have a residence. I've paid rent on it for three months to be told last week that I was case-staffed to max out of jail so technically I max in twelve weeks but doing so, I will lose my residence. Yeah!

So, I've sent a grievance number to central office two weeks ago, have heard nothing back as of yet. Last Monday, I sent a letter to prisoner's rights and today my attorney from P.R. came to discuss my case.

I don't care about maxing out, but I have seven children and three grandchildren. It's my granddaughter's first everything and I truly WANT to participate in all of it, not just see pictures and hear about everything.

Dammit, I've been sober for two years. I haven't picked up new charges. I have an apartment. I have means to support myself. I have a counselor set up, maintenance set up, a job, and education. I have a sponsor and a mentor. I'm currently working the twelve steps and I am in grief counseling. They let me out before with nothing set up; and now I'm ready but here I sit, kept from everything that's healthy for me.

THE STORY I'VE TOLD
A. Gab

You see, if I had to tell the story my way, I probably couldn't tell you much. Just when I think I might have a grasp, it slips right through my fingers and blows into dust. There has to be more than just dust. I wish that I could say that this story was a happy one…on the contrary, unfortunately. A young girl never stands a chance when she doesn't know how to swim and is forced to walk the plank. The ocean swell will suck you in quicker than you'd think, but not fast enough when you're drowning. After a struggle and a fight for air, a hand might pluck her out or she might just fight and hold on…does she give up? Sink or swim, there will be a fight. Just when her lungs are burning with fire, she begins to float to the surface hanging on to the life that's left…at this point it's not much. It never has been; but being consumed by this body of water has changed things. Colors appear different, words don't sound the same. Walking doesn't come naturally anymore. Everything is pushing against the will of the lost, little girl. No one is there to teach her new life. Left to her own devices, the story changes, never stays on track. So many times, it has been rewritten, so many times ripped up, so many times the words read wrong. Now what do you say when the end is near, and the last sentence is waiting to be written?

TO THE SYSTEM
Tess

I sit in a system that has far out-broken right from wrong, has long out-lasted its last facelift and has done little to sustain its swinging back door. My own body has been over-stimulated by this system, loudness echoes each corner of these walls. But does the system listen to the voices that vibrate along the bricks? Hoping ears become penetrated by whispers—do you care?

I am a mother of four children lost in a system. My mother was one of seven children all lost in a system. I've heard the stories about systems being enveloped by larger systems and those systems became so big they forgot their own mission statement.

I know when I'm not forced to be within this system, I have my own system. It's my own life system. I have a comfy couch I like to watch TV on. It longs to become used. When does the system give up? Who gives power to me and to women in positions that abuse it? Is there a secret system we don't dare to look at? I sit in a system that is fear, stuck in one that does not work.

I stood up last night and howled loudly, fear springing forward, knocking it over with the truth, hatred churning in the bellies of so many broken women.

WHAT IS HAPPENING?
Cindy

I am at an all-time low.
Total discourse is wearing me down.
My eyes burn from tears,
my body hurts all over,
especially my chest, my arms, my back.
I actually thought,
Is this how a heart attack feels?
I also thought, *Oh god,*
I can't take this abuse anymore.
People agitate and provoke you,
not only inmates but correctional officers.
I have begun to advocate
for relief from all the unfair cruelty
we are subjected to.
I have written to everyone from
the superintendent, to the central
office, even the risk reduction teacher.
I have involved all that I trust,
because something has to change.
A mentor would be nice.
Someone, anyone, a soul friend.
I keep telling myself to persevere,
follow the passion you feel.
Anything is possible.
Living here, a total life change for me.
How will I continue?
I don't even feel like a person.
The thought of my son and my grandchildren
keep me going. I am lost.
God is what is keeping me alive.
I don't even think that is what I want.

THEY SPEAK TRUTH TO POWER

Dylen

I believe jails need to gain more knowledge about inmates who identify differently than others. Transgender individuals seem to be getting incarcerated more and more. I feel that the staff here needs more training; using the excuse "this is a women's jail" is not OK. They need to respect that there are others around that may be different. Some staff genuinely care and others just shrug it off. Just because some people are inmates doesn't mean they are any less a person. If there are transgender inmates, they should give input and educate staff at trainings about issues like using gender-appropriate pronouns and general group-speak. Although there is now a policy in place, staff don't use it consistently.

To the Editor,
I believe jails need to gain more knowledge about inmates who identify differently than others. They need to train staff with the input of transgendered individuals who can help them understand the issues.

At this facility, some staff genuinely care while others shrug it off. But there is a policy about using gender-specific pronouns, yet staff don't follow the policy consistently.

It is time for staff to receive transgender-informed training and to be held accountable for the consistent application of policies.

PERMISSION
wiVT participant

Permission to breathe again.
Permission to live again.
Permission to breathe again.
(Permission to live again)

Permission from whom?
Permission when?
Permission for what?
Permission for how long?

I give myself permission to pause; to slowly come to a decision;
permission to change my mind.

I give myself permission to say 'no, thank you.' I give myself time to just
be, or to meditate. I give myself permission to waste time, waste money.

And I give myself permission to forgive myself for thinking and acting as
if I need permission to do anything.

Permission is imagined; it's controlling; waiting for it is what has held
me back and held me still, frozen in fear, frozen in time.

I give my son permission to hug, because he almost always asks first.
Then he says, 'this feels so good.'

I give my granddaughter permission to run in the house, just because.

I give myself permission to feel anything that comes up because I can
breathe now.

DARKNESS
Peggy Lee

Darkness ... what is that?
Haven't seen darkness for a bit!
Even when the lights go out here, you can still see shit!
I don't know the reason for always having light.
Truth be known, darkness would give the guards a fright!
It doesn't really matter to me, 'cuz I don't sleep much.
I guess that's because my family and I are outta touch.
If I ran this dump, and ran that light switch,
when it was time for bed, I wouldn't be a bitch!
I'd shut the lights off, for everyone to sleep.
Nobody would complain, I wouldn't hear a peep.
For if I could have just a little darkness maybe I could sleep
instead of lying there in the light with nothing to do but weep.

DISCONNECTED
wiVT participant

A funny story…I would usually be able to do this with ease except for the two-legged concrete walls trying to surround me…the funny thing being it all feels more and more like a joke on me. The past three years have been one big joke—eh. Crap. I am just not mentally showing up here. My laughter hasn't done much except antagonize the naysayers…what I write about tonight? I am unable to enjoy the laughter. It's been continually pecked away here and there. I feel riddled with holes and no longer know who the whole me is anymore. But there it doesn't matter—eh, ugh—I needed to end this day on a positive…funny—I am blank, my voice is froggy with asthma and my head hurts with the pointless envy of verbal escalated volleyballs thrown up, down, and around me. WTF again. A good day or two does not mean much more than that. I just wanna sleep, it's been a very long, very, long-long 34 hours…and it's not a joke but it is on me. But I am okay with the process, the act of what is now, for now…freeing from myself? That is the magic?

I am sorry I am disconnected tonight :)

It's a relief

FOR THOSE WHO DON'T SPEAK
Amber

I am writing for those women who don't like to speak and for those that don't have a voice because they are terrified to speak. We should not be scared to talk. We should say or think what we feel. Women are sometimes scared to speak or ask for help because people judge us too much. We can't say what's on our mind. But for me, I will speak. I will talk freely and don't care. We as women should not be scared to talk about anything.

HOWL
Sarah

What is my howl?
What I see every day: incarcerated brilliant minds, untapped potential, beat down by a system so unwilling to see the good.
What we all want: a breath of new life, a fighting chance.
These set-ups for failure are convenient at worst and very lucrative.
I can shout and shout, but when I'm locked in this cage, it seems no one can hear me. I know that you all can hear me, but where it matters, my message fall on deaf ears.
Conformity to me is sickening. I do not fit in a mold. My mind numbs at others' ability to march on, heads down, doing the same as the next, and so on.
I want us to all be the different that we are.
To conform, to be censored, to be colored in the lines, is to have lost my soul. You may as well strike me dead.
Ignorance may be bliss, as some say. But it is no sense of peace to me. I'd rather be intelligent to my loss than ignorant to my defeat.
And we sit here, locked in, we are not losing.
We must revolutionize our system. My words cannot be the only thing fighting against this.
I cannot be the only noise buzzing in the ears of our adversaries.
All this is can be delivered onto the people unto us.
We need to have a voice, to rise up.
Please, I implore you to make a change. Use your words make the point—use your voice to make the impact. Call me insane, but I will do it again and again. I will fight against, I will love, I will laugh. I will howl whenever necessary and will be prepared for any judgment as a result.
We can obtain the keys to our freedom.
The choice being, do we fight or simply wait?

LOSS AND LONGING

I SEE A LIGHT BUT FORGET
Tess

I've been stuck in the rain for hours, my hands grip the pole I am tied to, screaming. I've been yelling in hope someone hears my cries.

The blouse my mother dressed me in today is streaked with mascara and all I can think about is how she's going to yell at me for the mess I've made of my new shirt.

My school books lay scattered at my feet. I look at my brown shoe, and I'm alone, frightened. Maybe I should have studied harder, not skipped class.

I pull away using my weight as a leverage to break free of what binds me to this pole. I am damp and not strong enough to break free, my scream breaks my cries. I am helpless. I look at my books again. I forgot I was the last one out.

My paper is lined with everything but what I was to write about. I should have paid attention.

AN ORDINARY DAY
Cindy

My days will be far from ordinary when my feet are firmly planted at home. Everything will be different - floors, walls, rugs, furniture. I will finally enjoy being home, alone with my beautiful pets. Sleeping 'til I want to rise. My routine was to have a cup of tea first, then perking a wonderful blend of coffee, getting a bagel ready to toast. Watch a little news, read from one of the books that I have made a list of, now that I discovered authors and book titles I found, or that a friend advised since I found a new career as a librarian. My choices are many, my mind is full of ideas I have dreamed of.

But first, I want to relax, sit on my deck, watch nature. I have missed the birds and squirrels, even the little meadow moles. The sun peeping through the leaves, God smiling down on me. The grass growing greener every day. Then I will feel happy, smile for a good cause, sit back, take everything in.

That will be my ordinary day, doing things 'my way.'

NO ESCAPE
A. Gab

In a matter of seconds, it was over. The sound was deafening. The smell of gasoline and the taste of blood. Upside down, I came to a rest, wondering how bad it actually was.

Did I really want to know? Too much had happened for me to assess the damages from here. In a blur of words and color, I was whisked away into the unknown. It's funny how I always seem to find God when I'm in a pinch. Would He even listen to me? I was screaming prayers, just in case He wasn't near. This kind of thing doesn't happen to me. I always skate by with a smile on my face. Well, not this time. The price I pay, you ask?

Six years and two lives that will weigh on my conscience eternally. Really, what's six years when these people are no longer here to watch their family grow and blossom? There is no comparison. I fear that six years will never shed the skin of guilt that I wear. And to those on the outside looking in, no price I could pay would ever be enough. If I could tell you one thing with certainty, it is that like a demon, I live in the hell of my mind with no escape. Many times over, I have tried, but I give up. All the exits are blocked.

Is it an eye for an eye you all want? Blood for blood? What I live with has killed my heart, killed my spirit; even if not in a physical sense, I have died, too. You may not think it. I may not show it. But there are so many layers to be peeled back before you see the truth, that part of me is gone forever. But you can't kill who I've become.

MY BODY
L. Bell

My body remembers the gentle touch of my mother's hands and all the love she had to give me.

My body remembers the warm feeling of holding hands with another.

My body remembers my first real relationships and how good it felt to be loved.

My body remembers the birth of all my children and the joy I felt with every one of them.

My body remembers embracing them as they grew and letting them go to start their own lives.

HEROIN
A. Gab

Slamming doors to shackles and cuffs.
Recorded phone calls to read through mail.
Phone ringing to no one answering.
Having everything to having nothing.
You have taken everything from me.
You have changed me for the worse.
No sense of change, no remorse,
no guilt for what I've done.
No feeling, no love, just hate.
No kids, no family, no phone, no visits.
Lost everyone and everything because of you
and you still want more.

LIFE LINES

"When patterns are broken, new worlds emerge."
   wiVT participant

As I'm looking up into the sky,
Watching life pass me by,
Connecting all the stars I can see
That are laid out before me;
Hoping to see an image unknown
That shines to be shown
As a zipper flies by -
I see the Big Dipper in the sky.
As I look to you and say
'Things are strange that way;
When patterns are broken,
New worlds don't always emerge.
Even if your eyes are beaten
While you binge and purge
It just seems to happen that way
Throughout today and yesterday.'

ALL MY LIFE
Mary

All my life I've been dissolving myself. I have dissolved myself into the tiniest rain drop. A chocolate drop so small not even a butterfly could taste it. Or one drop out of a rain cloud that fell into the sea unnoticed, swallowed by the whale of DOC. It would cry out when a poacher took the last bit of air out of its massive lungs.

All my life I've been dissolving myself.
I can dissolve myself no more, not now…
now that I've dissolved myself into the tiniest rain drop
or a chocolate drop so small
not even a butterfly could taste it.

LOVE
Tess

From the gap between our aspirations and our behaviors, I have realized over the years I love you for the distance our love has created. It's given me the freedom to express myself in ways that move me forward.

Yet, we succumb to our habits and are left shaken from our distasteful behaviors. It is you in the quiet of my mind I think of. I dream big and my heart expands at the realization I've loved you for so so long – yet there's room to love you more. Every time I've pulled back the sheets and closed my eyes, it was you who I longed to be there with, a quiet, resting security in knowing you shared my darkness. You showered me in light and you took the star, making it brighter than any 3 am light bulb, blaring its hum-bum while I awoke to eat a bowl of cereal.

Your aspirations were always bigger than the life we lived and your actions backed up your passion for our love. I am blessed knowing it is us, not you, or just plain old me. It's us. The swing in our hips as we share a long stroll on the beach. It's us. The long nights sleepless while we fight our demons and renounce our right to another go around. It's us. Painting our home, placing the picture over the mantle that sparks our love for that special place where we sit. It's us that has long out lasted any misjudgment toward one another. It was worth every foot-stomping shout because without a doubt, you are the stronger and better half in my life; and when the odds are stacked up against me, it's you who pulls me through.

I miss your touch, the good morning kiss and the unknown whatever you made in my lunch bag. I miss facing you each night at a dinner table, sharing my day. I'm far more fearful sitting here each and every day, being forced to eat with strangers sometimes, not knowing what to say, pushing my food down, my fear not being able to push words out and just talk. I have taken so much for granted while you've given me every opportunity to listen and share my opinions with me and I've pulled away. It's the demon of a lonely heart that keeps me at bay, restless and sick. And it's this moment - right here - that reminds me that there's always an option. As long as I give my own heart the chance to become evolved into a strong, beating vessel, encouraged to fight this addiction and give in to a love so powerful that keeps me remembering I am loved. And I do love you.

MYSTERIOUS WOMAN
Sarah

Who are you, this mysterious woman holding a lifeline? Allowing me to fade into the background. Am I not enough, can you not see me or hear me? My lungs are devoid of air. I see a sign in the flames. You know what this is, a mixing and melding of thought. The electrons in your brain are firing, branching out into space and time. A dream, within a dream, within itself. Is it my mind reacting, am I this mystery woman? Holding my own lifeline tightly in my hands, listening, non-moving, not reacting to my very own cries for help? Should I turn around and look? What is this line tethered to and why am I holding it? This can't be right. Those pale eyes. They don't match the dark brown behind my glasses. I can't help but feel afraid. I am terrified of the unknown, the lack of control. Adrift in these fractals, with no sense of time. Numbers never end, will this? Will I always be yelling into this empty space? I am not one for hopelessness and despair. I just can't help but feel the cold fingers of sadness, when my eyes drift across this page.

STILL POSSIBLE
Melissa

Are you still possible?
You wild nexus of thought
and convergence with sleep
and hallucination, my
subconscious' view of
what am I to do with
this entirely crazy man
who seems uncomfortably
able to see me. Are you
dream, are you possible?
Is there some catalogue
of hope and possibility
that I've never run
across before? Did I
suddenly, at this late
stage, develop a fairy
godmother with a punk
rock aesthetic?
What is the world even
winding down to and
how am I ever going
to deal with how
bloody fucking confused
I am on a regular basis?

WHAT I'D LEAVE BEHIND
Cindy

I'd like to leave behind the noise,
leave behind the rude morning awakenings,
be done with hard beds and flat pillows,
never feel these cold floors again.
I long for a private bath.

Is this too much to ask for?
I want to cook my own food,
wash my own clothes,
clean my own home,
go to the market by myself,
drive my own car.
I want to leave behind this life here,
start anew - leave anxiety behind.
I want to say Happy New Year
and be the courageous woman I am.

MY PAINTING
wiVT participant

The painting I did tonight reminds me of when I got married. When I got married, it was a beautiful sunset over the vineyard. The waterfall was the noise in the background. The trees were swooshing in the wind, the sky was a light orange and the air was a warm touch. I got married on August 30, 2005. The reason I wanted to paint that day is because that was the happiest day I could remember with a beautiful sunset.

Every August, we both stop and look at the sunset and remember that wonderful night, and how happy we both were to see such an amazing sight.

I paused in this moment to become happy once again.

I wanted to put my wife and I in the sunset painting, but I am not very good at painting or drawing people, so I just imagined us being there together.

MY BODY REMEMBERS
A.D.

My body remembers that life and cries for the lost parts of itself when it comes to the things I've been forced to go through.

My body remembers that life and cries for the lost parts of itself when it comes to my childhood.

My body remembers that life and cries for the lost parts of itself when I was using.

My body remembers that life and cries for the lost parts of itself when I lost everything and everyone when I was using.

My body remembers that life and cries for the lost parts of itself when I lost my mother.

My body remembers that life and cries for the lost parts of itself when I came to jail.

My body remembers that life and cries for the lost parts of itself when I was forced to deal with change.

SEEKING SILENCE
Cindy

I long for quiet, peace,
like sitting on an empty beach
only hearing the sounds of nature.
Instead, all I hear is constant bickering,
noise beyond my control.
What is this place?
A playground of yelling,
a room of screaming women?
Is it just me? Why don't they all just shut up?
No one seems to be in charge
of this group of wild maniacs.
I'm sorry if I sound cranky.
I'm too old for this way of living.
Hopefully, soon, I will experience
each day as a sacred gift.

SAFE LOVE CHALLENGED
Louise

Earth conceals its spin by spinning me with it,
so much going on. No foundation
under the house; a fractured heart;
confusion, harsh words
and very tired hand.

Joy, loss, love, yearning --
struggle and constraint --
knowledge, strength,
broken heart, hurt smile.
Big change. My hairs
go singly gray only by night.

CHANNELING THE GIRL
Tess

I am a little girl who stands alone, uncomfortable, unable to play. I feel restricted to play freely due to the dress my mother made me put on this morning. I would have rather worn a pair of my favorite jeans that were passed down to me by my third oldest brother. I've been watching my brother's ball tap off his head in rapid succession for months now. He's gotten really good at keeping the ball from hitting the pavement. I know in my mind I should be the girl who wears the old faded pair of jeans with the left knee ripped out, just to show that even though I sit here and watch, I can bounce the ball off my head just as good. Oh, how it would feel to prove I've been watching and have learned. I, too, can play just like my brother, even if I have to be embarrassed in my new uncomfortable pastel peach dress.

NORMALIZING THE ABNORMAL
Dani

The mind is such an amusing organ. Not amusing as in a funny show or a jester drawing the attention of royalty.

Amusing as a perfect reason to be imperfect. Just when you believe yourself to be complacent, something comes around to tear apart your self-appointed magnificence. It's amazing what a person can survive.

Every kind of pain listed with check marks next to them like a roll call of every undeserving tear, yet the smallest of battles and she loses the ability to thrive. I've woken up at the age of 12 when most are hoping to go to the movies past 10 pm. My abortion had been done in time to catch the bus.

At 17, I lived alone, my daughter, a cat, and rent all looking at me. For what? Sometimes I wasn't sure, but the cat liked the milk. I gave the baby so much it chewed most of her bottles up.

By 21 I had three kids and no one to help us but I didn't mind. I worked every day, sun up to sun down, with no fuss. My girls deserved the world and I had no shame.

My spiritual integrity broke the day I joined the game.

I've become a broken record playing the mishap, mishap, playing the mishaps over again. My insecurities grow like a seed that was put in this pot in a garden with razor wire holding out the smile in the pain. I miss being just a little rain. I miss the tiny hugs that made me feel loved by the ones whose eyes gave me the shine to begin with. Why can't I keep that as my normal?

I'd like to abnormalize my normal but my normal is abnormal so how will I know which normal is normal because abnormal sure feels normal to me?

LABORING is in my blood. The hustle, as most call it, is nothing but lame. I was as good at selling drugs as Helen Keller was at coloring in the lines.

And before I knew it, I was paying Vermont restitution and fines, 260 lbs, and confidence to fill a truck.

Carpenter, chef, photographer, landscaper, Carnie, a little blarney deserved. All that said I've dealt with some shit. And dealt with it all smiling. Okay, maybe my teeth were grit.

Beat, raped, overworked, and alone. Sometimes I didn't have a home. I was fine with a smile but here, this place can kill the light inside. A woman who unequivocally valued herself became fearful of her thoughts.

Ashamed of her weight when she'd never been in a physically different state. Her once impermeable thoughts became bended and worn. What is normal?

In order to solidify, you must stop being so vulnerable. I never knew that I could feel this way again. Normalizing normal is harder than normalizing a bad habit. It was easy to pick up a needle, become used, washed up, and frail, yet an AA meeting or playing a sport can be worth picking on someone. You get teased for being a good person here.

You get laughed at for having manners. How can it be "normal" to laugh at someone with scars on her fragile arm because of some sad, underlying reason, to viciously take it out on every kind, sad, equally broken soul around you.

HOPE AND FEAR
Emily

Hope is better than fear, optimism better than despair.

I know these things. I know them and I repeat them over and over. But their application is elusive. The hope of being whole and able does not drive me. Rather the fear of falling apart moves me to action. But the pieces are breaking apart faster than the hands can stitch them together. So I work faster in an attempt to limit the fall. What happens when it all falls apart? What happens to me when the pillars of my strength crumble? What will be left of me? Fear drives. Fear of despair, of submission, of defeat. Faster, I have to patch the cracks up faster. Stitch the wounds, quickly before my life bleeds too much. Here's a band-aid. Here's some tape. You're breaking apart, jam it back together. Juggle, juggle, fix, don't fall … oh, yeah - and breathe! Don't be afraid, hope! I am afraid to hope. I am afraid of what comes when hope fails. I am a Picasso all patched together. This is not art. This is pain.

Hope is better than fear, but harder to come by.

STUCK
Amber

Stuck in jail with no bail.
Friends I had no longer exist,
only my fellow convicts.
I got dragged to the box on the daily,
wishing I could just be with baby.
All I do is resist and get major's,
loving life in danger.
A1's on cops, too many to count,
sitting in my tin box, living in doubt
of ever getting out.
I don't know why I keep freakin'.
I should just stop speakin'
but I can't, it's impossible.
This fight I have is internal like a hot inferno
taking over my entire being.

THE FLAMMABLE YEAR
Melissa

If I could, I would burn away
so many things from this old year.
The weight of day upon day, hanging
stiff and heavy on my back like
textbooks guilting me for not learning
whatever this godforsaken course
is supposed to cover, backpack
slapping against my ribs at every step.
The hopelessness of one, the guilt at
another, the never-after of a third,
and none of them quite suitable,
but don't I just love me some guilt?
Maybe I should burn all of that up
for one of those ridiculous New Year's resolutions,
but no one keeps those and it does
add a nice spice to a dish the
universe seems bent on serving cold.
The year itself, surprisingly enough,
still not the worst year of my life,
but oh, what I wouldn't give to
watch it curl and writhe in the flames,
burn, baby, burn! It's one of those
years I'm not sure should be saved
in a bottle, except I would even
spend bad years to have the years
in my hands to be spent.

HAVE TO HAVE LAUGHS
wiVT participant

Can't live without it.
My friends and I laugh our necks off.
All day long - long neck, short neck,
fat neck, skinny neck. I love all necks, chub neck, stub neck.
Sara neck, Deb neck, Tasha neck, Diamond neck -
we are the toughest necks in town.

I feel like laughter is the best medicine.
It's something I have to have. It's
something I crave. I have to have
it. Without it I can't survive. I
need people like me
that laugh their necks off.
Great white shark necks.

FLASHBACK

an in-class group writing

I strained to decipher
the bright lights dilating your eyes.
Years erased any trace of my existence,
an unending view in the mirror.
Scary was my first thought.
I breathed faster than normal.
I couldn't banish the deep heavy feeling -
the sound of a dentist's drill,
the low tones that might have been moaning.

This is a hard question to answer,
mesmerized by my imagination.
He drilled, it seemed, for hours
the throbbing drone of a chainsaw.
Infinite trails of thought sent me reeling;
stripped of my hard exterior,
another hand had reached into my soul.

I was not a secret.
I tried not to breathe.
I forced myself to move on.
The only alternative was unacceptable to me.
You have never witnessed a place all despise.
All I wanted was out.

HOME AGAIN
Ashley

It's been almost a year. I smile just thinking I'll soon be back in the swing of things. Mommy, my favorite word. To hear it come from those little mouths is simply breath-taking. Adham is another year older and dislikes the Ninja Turtles and loves Power Rangers now. Gee! I remember the re-do of his room. Mohamed and I stayed up late one birthday for him just to fix his room up in everything Ninja Turtle. My mom and him had the adventures this time. Everything is Power Rangers. My Mom sent me information on all of them. I better read up just to know who's who, especially the Gold One with his powers! He is almost done with his first year of school.

And Uoseff starts next year. My babies are growing. He's out of the big kid pull-ups and wears the little boxers on his little butt. I have missed running my fingers through them jet black curls. Just laying all cuddled up and his beautiful hazel eyes gazing up at me. And my baby Selim is no longer a baby.

CREATIVITY WITHIN

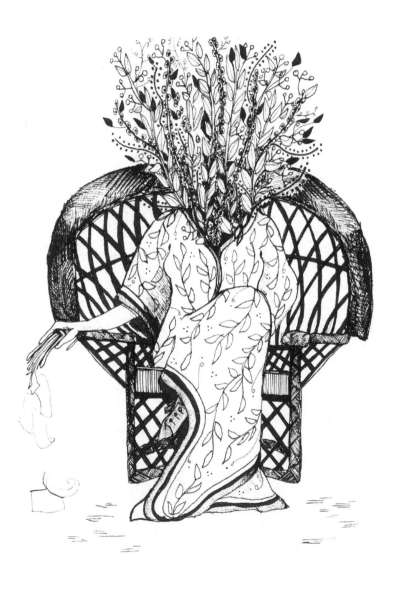

"Let things happen rather than make them happen."
　M. Ga

During this practice, we used the flimsy string to draw in India ink. The ink will stain whatever it touches and the utensil that is being used to guide the ink where it may go doesn't offer a definite outcome. Knowing the ink is going to fall where it wants and that it will remain in its place signifies the lack of control of our life's outcome; yet, we are still in charge of the motions to make certain that it happens. "Whatever we do in life will be insignificant, but it's important that we do it."

We call this art - "the conscious use of skill or imagination." If we wanted to, we could use colors that were a bit more promising - markers, crayons to fill in the otherwise abstract areas of our pieces.

We are not the authors of this world; we are not our own creators. We all are going through the motions of life. Sometimes we fight our fate, when we realize that everything has already fallen where it's supposed to against our will. We are just color in the void. We are at peace. We have the power to contribute but not to control.

TRICKED
Cindy

I am the correctional gestapo, Klinko,
in charge of you three men.
Pay close attention, this is opportunity.
Henry, Marvin, Keith.
You will be given three choices.
They could be good, bad, or evil.
First, Henry you must go into the woods.
Pick Marvin to accompany you.
Marvin, you will give Keith a firearm.
Keith, your choice is to pick what
you want cooked for supper.
Second, follow the corn maze, separate
from each other,
pick one item in the corn maze.
Lastly, you will open the first door
you find that is painted red.
Henry runs outside, stumbles and as
he enter the corn maze,
he falls through a black hole.
Klinko laughs hysterically.
That was easy, no more Henry,
now there are two.
Marvin and Keith find a dark room

filled with sophisticated firearms,
all loaded and ready to go.
He picks the biggest, most powerful
machine gun, and hands it
to Keith who immediately
begins to hunt for supper.
He finds the biggest bison he
ever saw and shoots it.
So happy, he found dinner.
Marvin meanwhile found a red door.
He entered and realized he had
turned into a wild animal.
Immediately, he was shot dead.
Klinko laughs hysterically.
One down the giant blank hole
never again to return. *Bye bye Henry.*
One turned into a buffalo
killed dead, never again to return,
Bye bye Marvin.
Now Keith, I have chosen you
to be my lover.
Keith cries hysterically
while Klinko just laughs.

THE DOORS
wiVT participant

As I walk down the long hallway of my apartment building, passing all my neighbors' doors, I stumble as I'm passing the third one on my floor. So, I approach it closer, I hear a strange but distinct noise. It's an erratic pounding sound with nothing else to be heard. Walking past, I find myself asking this question in my thoughts . . . "What could be the cause of that dreadful sound in there?!"

However, I choose to mind my own business and proceed down the hall to my apartment. But much to my surprise, just two doors down, another sound catches my attention . . . The sound of a high-pitched whine of machine draws me close to the door. So close, in fact, that my ear is pressed up against the cold metal door, which sends shivers down my spine. Once my ear is pressed against the door, another sound catches my attention on what might be going on on the other side of that door. As I continue to listen, the newfound sound becomes even clearer to me. It's the sound of laughter.

Realizing the sound, I back away from the door and continue to my apartment. I approach my door and as I'm searching my purse for my keys, I hear another sound. This time, the sound is coming from my apartment. Standing at my door, frozen to this finding, I'm unable to move. Moments later, still frozen, my door swings open with the sound of "surprise!" shouted toward me. The look on my face causes those inside to burst out laughing at one another. Meanwhile, I start weeping at the thought of all my family inside my apartment waiting for my arrival. Now unfrozen from my puzzlement, all those other sounds behind those other doors were wiped away. All I heard now was the sounds of love and joy coming from the other side of the door. Only this time, I was making the sounds I heard.

PAUSE AND LOOK
Cindy

Under the sky of orange, yellow and red,
it mimics itself on the mountains.
I pause and can't stop looking
at the beauty of the melting colors.
They blend like a watercolor painting.
The tips of the mountains,
evergreens dancing in wind.
I pause again and look below.
Ripples of blue water.
They mesmerize me like a fire.
I Listen to the wind.
The birds are singing just for me.
A Vision I'll always remember,
sounds I'll never forget --
my own nature in my mind.

THE WORLD ROLLS
Melissa

The world rolls in chaos
       like a dog through skunk carcass
       in jubilation for getting filthy with
       scandal, slaughter, war and shame.
The world rolls in chaos
       like a child on a fragrant summer hill
       stained and scraped, rumpled clothes and
       scuffed shoes, wearing the evidence.
The world rolls in chaos
       like a child and winter's first snowman
       gathers mud, leaves and stubborn grass,
       contaminating snowy creation.
The world rolls in chaos
       like a baker rolls a dessert
       through powder and shreds of shattered lives
       adding flavor, sweetness and decoration.
The world rolls in chaos
       like a tank across a killing field
       soulless mechanical destruction marches
       anything but blindly, scenting blood.
The world rolls in chaos
       like a corpse into a shallow grave
       meaty facedown thud screams
       guilt, corruption, sin and cessation.

MY FEET REMEMBER
   Cindy

It is spring, but today there was snow
on the ground.
As I looked out my frosted window,
white covered the dead grass,
when will you turn green?
I am waiting patiently.
I want my feet to feel soft blades
coming out of the earth.
I can't wait for my feet to feel
soft white beach sand.
Fall and Winter are now a thing
of the past.
Unfortunately, my feet didn't have
the chance to walk on crunchy
Autumn leaves.
My feet wanted to feel the fluffy
cold flakes of winter.
That didn't happen either.
I do feel a glimmer of hope
that this spring and summer
will be different.
This could be a pipe dream.
I believe there is still a chance
for my feet to be free again,
for they know the
seasons by heart.
A legend of four winds blowing
belong to me and you.
Patiently, we wait for another world to start.

THE SCENT AS IT WILL BE (excerpt)
  wiVT participant

Alone, tending the stove
ignoring the babbling,
the crackling and screaming,

tending the stove
I stir three times.
I am reading

thirsty for the world,
thirsty for knowledge,
thirsty to fly away...

ALMANAC
Dani

When I think of an almanac, I think of an old farmer knee deep next to the pit, you know the one with the conveyor belt delivering the next load of, we could say scat, I guess; but he's staring up to the sky wondering if that woolly bear caterpillar he stepped on earlier was right. Spring's coming but is it really time to spread that … scat? Well, knee high by July, we barely have time to reap what we sow. An almanac of last things …what's more last than some scat?!

DRAGON DANCE
Valerie

Dancing to a discordant melody
in the pale moonlight darkness
I did not care to see
I was dancing with the dragon's carcass.

Then there you were, walking
in the shadows. My broken porcelain eyes
could see without struggle or hesitation
you heard the same melody!

Painted branches make up the tree
of Hope and Dreams where gods are fools
and cats say, *Yes, Miss Alice.*

With castles, clouds and golden dreams
nothing is as it seems, where the rabbit hole
never ends, nor does the chalice.

None of that matters, for you are here.
Knowing better, I fall. Let me know you,
let me near. Still, you don't hear.
You won't hear my silent call.

I can't have you, but still you feel me.
I pick up the dragon's carcass and soar.

My photos burn in their glitter frames
my heart still beats, apparently. I laugh —
but smile no more. This is my song.
This my dance. This makes no sense.
Welcome to my trance.

DON'T HIDE AWAY, MY PRINCESS
wiVT participant

Don't hide away my princess,
come out when you're not stressed.
Don't hide away my princess,
come out and meet your guest.
Don't hide away my princess,
come out and look your best.
Don't hide away my princess,
the prince is wearing his vest.
Don't hide away my princess,
come mingle on my request.
Don't hide away my princess,
we would like to see your dress.
Don't hide away my princess,
you are starting to become a pest.
So, go ahead and hide away,
hide from your guest.
Hide from your prince.
Don't look your best.
Don't wear that dress.
Don't even look this way.
Go ahead and hide away!

MY TREE
Dani

Whenever I sit down to relax and draw something nice,
it never really seems to change.
I keep drawing the same dying tree, like it's my vise.
Not as if my vision has a wide range;
as you'll clearly see,
this place is definitely no paradise.
A sunset, not always the best.
Not one has had the apple that hangs to the right.
Isn't that a little strange?
I've drawn it so much; a blindfold test would prove it tonight.
I bet the shading and details were perfected even without my sight.
At times, my repetition is nothing short of dullness.
Maybe it's more an underlying issue, making my hands
keep them in store.
An immense canvas which I will never finish,
continuously creating the same project until I diminish
focusing on what I may have left out.
Maybe that's what it is,
waiting for the day my painting can tell you every word
I'm trying to shout,
or maybe it should never be finished.

WHAT IS HERE
Mary

Eyes, blue
hair, brown
girl, friend
mine, always
mine, girl
gone, empty
world, soul
haunted, love
gone, fears
shed, days
long, time
spent, help
brown, heart
ache, pain
empty, cells
call, home.

BEYOND THE HORIZON
Melissa

The line I called
the horizon
does not exist.
It's somewhere back on the
twentieth floor or so. I cling
to brass bars and press
my back to the paneling as
acceleration crushes
fear of discovery. I creep
toward sweeping fragility,
hope of the familiar
vanished. A man in a
bottle green velvet suit sings
about a heart he left in
North Billerica, of all the
unlikely places. The city
spins itself forever

from gray and black
cotton candy blur. Rain
beats and tower
sways. My eyes are
glued - sturdy framework,
desperately reassuring,
rain isn't leaking in,
glass doesn't spontaneously
shatter from fear. A
customer spirits away
five years growth,
a highball glass,
detonates on tile
two booths down. A slap
of phosphorescent white towel
on black marble bar is
almost as frightening.
"What'll it be tonight?"
    "The usual."

THE FIELD
    Dani

Behind the house I grew up in
is a giant field.
A sea of dandelions
the rippling tide that could swallow me whole.
When I think about a time
I could really smile about:
I've walked the eternity
across the green ocean.
Poseidon at my heels
to the back corner where
the hills are.
If every thought I had was
a blade of grass
and every tear I shed
a dandelion, I'd fill this field twice over.
And now I'm grown,
trespassed
back to my sanctuary,
swimming in the tear of Gaia.
If I sit, the grass hides
my lonely presence,
eaten by mother Earth's child.
I lie in my newly forbidden getaway,
staring up at the stars
as if I had never left,
never grown up,
never felt pain,
never knew dysfunction,
never had to walk back across the field.

SWELLING DARKNESS
Melissa

Each generation grows darker, daughter by daughter.
Reckless tsunami of poison in our veins.
We curse the earth we're born to walk,
shadow-seek, hiding from sun's burning source.
Wreak destruction in an avalanche from a single stone.
What restless insect wing brought about the hurricane?
Which grinning demon spit in the well of our creation?
Daughter by daughter, putrefaction poured out,
a gathering of lost sinners in a single strand of mitochondria.
We, women of pain, women of the end of all things.
We are family, after all.

DANSE MACABRE
Valerie

Into the night, she dances
a dark bird in glittering moonlight.
If darkness dare dream,
it would dream of her
a speck of unattainable light,
a dream within a dream.
Afraid to touch, afraid to spoil
this beauty in darkness,
the only one to find beauty in decay
undistracted, in her own world.
What would you do?
Danse macabre in the depths
of the zodiac blindly with her
eyes bandaged but her aura receiving.
Castles, clouds and golden dreams.
Nothing else is as it seems
as they dance silently into the night.
Nothing else is as it seems
as they dance silently into the night.
She writes in the darkest ink I've ever seen.
She is screaming until her soul is clean
for someone, somewhere, leaving a scar
that she rubs from time to time.
Someone, somewhere crossed the line
and the truth has left her blind.
If she ever dreams of letting go,
this is what she'll need to do:
Let go all the lies that tore her world apart.
Forget every "I love you" that's scarred her heart.
Subdue this savage heart that cannot be tamed.
Let go of all these burning photos in their glitter frames.

GREAT AMERICAN SHOWS
Dani

I wandered in a land where I knew no one.
My whole life flipped and undone,
I landed on an island of misfits — adult-style.
And I fit in more and more
with every traveled mile.
There was the man that ran the Ferris wheel, the real deal.
Sitting on a carousel on my break
after 14 hours of funnel cakes
and sandwiches of cheese and steak.
Carnies can be a hell of a time.
They'd do anything for you
at the drop of a dime.
I can build a tilt-a-whirl in three hours flat
or play a game with a ball and a bat.
A clown named Smiley who never
drops character. We're family regardless.
There's nothing but laughter.

RELATIONS
Mary

Dilating	Shine
Shrink	Embrace
Shrink	Embrace
Insane	Behold
Insane	Behold
Mindless	Discover
Mindless	Discover
Aloof	Declare
Aloof	Declare
Standby	Dictate
Standby	Dictate
Patience	Rule
Patience	Rule
Virtue	Defiance
Virtue	Defiance
Compassion	Purpose
Compassion	Purpose
Empathy	Embody
Empathy	Embody
Emotion	Assemble
Emotion	Assemble
Expression	Enfigure
Expression	
Difference	
Difference	
Standout	
Standout	
Shine	

WISE WOMAN'S WORK
Tess

A long time ago, a poison seeped into my lungs, suffocating me. It took me without sorrow for how it affected my spirit. This poison was beautiful. She was a mother of pearl. So strange she could pull me out of any subcutaneous realm. She would awaken my sense to wander. Peering through blown glass, I could dance to the rhythm that took. She would only fight me when the night fell to darkness and chased away my light. She took my eyes so I couldn't see. She took my heart so it didn't beat. They become hers and not mine. Her temper would flare like rockets so high in the sky, it would rain hopeless anger on those who stood by in waiting. At times, it was so hard for her to live inside me because she had to manipulate my palette for the things that I craved. Many times I dominated her. I would look away, regain my eyesight and gradually begin to struggle back into awareness. I was drawn to her. She gave me moonless nights filled with obstacles. On nights like those I tamed her and gave her purpose and would dig deep down. The wise woman's work was never too late to be done. The love she had savored was pure; its violent beating heart expanded with every loving thought that was ever good within her temple. Suddenly she transformed, she began to drink from the well of life, eating from the branches that reached out to her. And she began to see her own reflection in the things she sowed. She cut her hair, trimmed her nails and quieted the beast. Now she sings lullabies to herself to pass the quiet times away. She remembers the cold streets, the empty nights, and builds on the dreams she once knocked down. She has risen. After falling so long, she counts the hairs that stand up and wishes them all well. She has a name:

— *Survivor* —

She is the one I feed.

HALF-DESTROYED INSTRUMENTS
Melissa

Never right, a dependable wrong,
not like a stopped clock
right twice a day, but always
incorrect, dutifully off the mark.
A by-word, it becomes, that
my sextant and astrolabe
are entirely useless for
plotting my course to anywhere
but fairyland, and
my fouled compass points
only to my own destruction.
I keep track, very precise
in measure, of how far
I've fallen, a log written
exclusively in my blood,
thinned for easy penning
with my tears and indignation.
I've tried to find a guiding star,
a bright beacon in the heavens.
But I find my life
has been far too cloudy for
any such bastion of proper navigation
to waste so much as
a thimbleful of stardust
on my poor wandering.

A TIME OF MAGIC
Patricia

Leaves fall from the trees outside, with blue-gray skies hovering above. I sit at peace within myself as I casually observe these changes. The air is cool and brisk. This is the season of corn and scarecrows, bats and black cats, pumpkins and trick-or-treating around the neighborhood. A time when we huddle around and watch scary movies about masked men and evil spirits, haunted houses and zombies. A time when the decorated houses seem to come alive with eerie lights and spider webs. And in every dark corner you come across, you hold your breath in playful suspense. No matter your age, you are destined to find something 'fun' to do when this time of year arrives. Haunted houses, haunted hay rides, ghost tours, ghost stories, scary movies … when you can eat pumpkin pies and sometimes what's watching you is none other than a few 'pumpkin spies' with scary grins and glowing insides. Where witches' potions and splintered notions of what is real and make-believe become hard to separate. And that is part of the magic of this beautiful time of year.

SAVING STRING
Cindy

Walking to Grandma's and Grandpa's
was just a stone's throw away
out the garden gate, past the neighbors
down the street, skipping. Everyone
knew my family in our close-knit neighborhood,
everyone waved and said 'hi.'
After church, the whole crew gathered
to have a cup of coffee, a shot of brandy
or a delicious slice of pastry or pizza.
The brown boxes, tied with love
from the Italian bakeries lined up on the counter.
As family and friends arrived,
Grandpa turned down the volume
on the radio playing Italian songs.
The platters were stacked.
The boxes were opened.
Young and old, we loved this Sunday tradition.
Grandma so happy, everyone came.
The kids made plates with pizza and treats.
All were cut in half so we could experience a lot.
We would go into the parlor and sit
on the new couch and chairs, always covered
with plastic. *Mangia! Mangia!*
Don't let it go to waste!
It was a time I'll never forget,
people I'll never forget, food I still crave
and the happiness everyone felt. But mostly,
in my heart and in my mind is

my beautiful Grandma's smile; and Grandpa
tucking the box strings in the drawer.

FRANKENSTEIN'S SOUL
Melissa

Re-member myself, shards and shreds,
    do explore those ancient accounts,
    dig up catacombs, read the
    inscription.
Is some part of my severed soul,
    buried here, in this rank earth,
    swampy and festering, rot
    pervading?
Will I find lost innocence
    moldering peacefully --
    a long-forgotten graveyard,
    mine to claim?
Once I find these bits and bobs,
    all the gewgaws and furbelows,
    can I sew them together
    back to me?
Can my shattered shadow join
    to itself, run together like drops
    of water pool, my parts drawn
    by Earth's pull?
Or will Shadow, strong as I,
    free at last with all her feathers,
    fly and drag this weak meat suit
    to tattered bits?
And, tattered, weak and weighty
    ribbons fall away, truly freeing,
    I too soar, re-membered, I
    don't fear flight.

IN THE BEGINNING
Cindy

God, I believe is one of us.
He created us as beings.
He wanted us to trust Him,
Adam and Eve were young, curious.
They wanted to be good
because they were so happy.
All they had to do was to think of something
and Poof! They received it.
Food, sun, breeze,
gardens with no weeds,
flowers blooming constantly.
There was no worry, no anxiety,
just, pure bliss.
Who could ask for anything more?
Until, a serpent walking,
wearing serpent skin boots approached beautiful Eve.
Who by the way, didn't have an ounce
of fat on her.
The slick serpent said to Eve,
May I walk with you?
Of course, you are very beautiful
and look so kind, your eyes
are glowing and your skin shimmers.
I have never seen anyone like you.
As they walked together,
Eve was mesmerized.
They strolled by this wonderful tree
and with no thought

the serpent plucked two
ruby red apples with a glimmer
of emerald showing through.
They just took a nice bite and,
oh, it was so delicious,
immediately, Eve realized
she had been scammed.
The once-good-looking serpent
turned ugly.
So ugly, she began crying.
Adam, Oh Adam, where are you?
I have been tricked.
The serpent made me bite the apple,
the one that was forbidden.
Adam didn't know what to do.
So, to calm Eve, he too bit the apple.
Suddenly, a flaming glow
came down from the sky:
See that serpent, he will never
walk again, just crawl on his
belly for eternity
and for the two you,
nothing will ever be easy again.
You had it made,
but didn't believe me.
I am one of you
but I am the Almighty.
You will suffer
and you will never win the lottery.

A TO Z
Emily

Astonishing, how Before the Children Danced Enthusiastically and Free, Gathered against Hearts once Ignorant to such Jovial Kaleidoscopes of Love. Motherhood meant Nothing. Only Petite fingers Quivering against a mother's breast. Reveal the Sacred bond that Trumps all things in this Universe. Valiantly the World simultaneously shrinks and Xpands, Yielding the true Zest of this life.

NAMES
Melissa

<u>Melissa</u> - given, vaguely acceptable, nearly unbearable when paired with "sweet," FUCK, do I hate the Allman brothers.
<u>Missy</u> - not if you want to live through the encounter unscarred by the sharp side of my tongue.
<u>Mel</u> - a friend, a close friend, might call me this way, after nights of drinking and music and prowling through life together.
<u>Legs</u> - They used to go on forever, back when I weighed 160 pounds or so, but only one old bastard's still standing who gets to call me that one.
<u>Annie Mack</u> - that's an old one, almost resurrected from a fossil, a remnant of a design career that went nowhere, killed by Vermont's cold and stubborn insistence on buffalo plaid and camo.

SONNET IV
Cindy

I love the smell when you cook:
garlic, onions, parsley, sage.
It never gets old. Follow the book:
tomatoes, basil, smell the rage.

Open the window. Turn on the fan.
Let the aroma fill the air.
The steam as you stir in the pan.
Your neighbors will think, "that's not fair."

I love to try different things
like mixing spices with sour cream.
Something good to put on those wings
will surely make you beam.
Take a bite. It will delight, yes.
Take a bite. It will delight, yes.

THE SOUND OF YOU
Dani

So, this is the sound of you
laughing as though a hyena
had just seen a baby elephant fall.

So, this is you happy
prancing around as if a good witch
in a bubble on your way to Oz.

So, this is your smile
glowing like a candle behind
the pumpkins grim grin.

So, those are your girls
loving you like you'd never walked away.
So, these are your tears, salty
as the deepest sorrows in the ocean.
So, this is your time
serving as a debt to your weaknesses.

So, these are your creations
painting worlds around yourself
like your daughter's greatest teacher.

So, these are your eyes, seeing
what was wrong. No more justifying pain.
So, this is almost you.

YOUR WEIRD GIRL
Melissa

I had a dream and you
were in it. I still
don't know why I cheered
when you decked his ass,
except maybe I felt like
you were my knight —
but your armor's not
shiny. It's showing some wear.
You laugh and tell me
I'm your weird girl.
Screams out across all
our conversations and
we haven't even touched yet,
and I'm still not sure
if you're looking forward to
soup, bread, and conversations
over cigarettes smoked
while I'm some variety
of yoga upside-down or
sex more.
You laugh and call me
your weird girl.
I listen to you spit fire
and labor organization,

proposing near-radical
activism, and I plan
soup and hot cocoa and fingerless
gloves so we can smoke and I
can take pictures of protests
to prove they happened even if
you're an utter Luddite and
I'm surprised your phone
isn't ten pounds of bakelite.
You laugh and say
I'm your weird girl.
I tell you about the royal
ruling class and how I
won't let it stand, even if it
is just a little thing and
you tell me about Knights
of Columbus and doughnuts
of privilege, and I say,
"Yes! Exactly!"
You laugh fondly and say
I love you weird girl.

WHEN PATTERNS ARE BROKEN

"You're always with yourself, so you might as well enjoy the company."
- Diane Von Furstenburg
    A. Gab

What part of me do you possibly think is good company to keep? Let me tell you as cleanly as I know how -I am not good company, I will be that demise, my own worst enemy. A scratching within that is never fully satisfied, a portal in my mind that takes me straight to hell. Constant reruns of the black-out scenes whisper and pull at my heart, leaving that aching and throbbing ever noticeable and constant. My skin would crawl away if I'd let it. With nowhere to go, it's been an intimately filthy knowledge of myself that I can say I never knew. All clouds lifted, I have looked into crevices I never knew existed, frightened and shaken. The only thing that keeps my feet still, planted like roots, is locked doors and barred rooms. I have nowhere to run and I sit feeling the growing resentment in my core. Time has brought some epiphanies, a revelation here and there. It doesn't bring me closer to myself. I wish I could say it did. The company I kept I can no longer. Now I'm left with just me.

I can't say this was my plan. I know it's not exactly working. I have never had the best answers. Now, I'm trying to find my way back to myself.

MOM
Valerie

I want to show the world how precious you were to me.
I want to show, with perfect precision, methodical strokes, how abstract
my world has become.
But I can't.
You made mothering look so peaceful, so harmless,
Even while trying to harness my adolescent emotional lava, too hot
for this chasm of a body.
You took every, "I hate you" in stride and every "I love you" with pride.
You're every part of me I love. You're everything I strive to be.
So, tell me, mom, where do I turn when there's no one left to blame
but me?
Well, it's time to put my big girl skin on now and be the ME you
intended me to be :)

HARBORED ALONE
Dani

It wasn't 'til that lonely night,
I realized I was alone,
so dark, so cold, so scary,
not a soul would pick up their phone.
I walked until I really lost sight
of where I might have gone.
The cold was getting so much worse.
I was frozen to the bone.
My dad said he couldn't;
my mother might find out.
Nothing would change that mind,
not even a world-famous pout.
I showed up on the porch anyways about 2 am.
I couldn't knock at that time.
It would only make anger to wake them.
I crawled in my father's shed
with my only real friend doing laps in my head.
I dug through my purse then I set up a camp
and started the process with light from a lamp.
Needle in hand, spoon, snow, and dope,
it's the only way to survive, a terrible way to cope.
That night I got high.
I was so scared when I almost died.
No one would've known where to look,
no one to help revive.
I hope now that's over.
I plan to do this on my own.
Isn't that what you're supposed to do
when you're grown?

DEAR MAMA-MAMA
Jayden

I would just describe her as an extraordinary yet ordinary woman.

Mama Mama, you're a star, a damn star.
Mama, remember when I lived in my car?
When I took the street shit too far?
How you always allowed me to come home?
You never gave up. You just loved me so hard.
Mama Mama.
You're the realist; I was always on the corners
making those deals, had to call collect
and you let me have it, always told me how you feel
and still do, although we shared many tears
and fears - the most common one was one
of us dying from our addiction, Mama.
You always prayed I wouldn't get killed.
My mama-my mama, you're my world.
You taught me how to win and not be a loser.
I know I used to tell you, "I hate you,"
but really, I'd hate to lose you.
Mama Mama, I know I'm incarcerated,
missing Mother's Day. I'm sorry Ma,
but I'll be alright. I really tried Mama… I still am.
Now that I'm older I regret
all the times I lied, didn't help none.
Mama your baby boy loves you.
You have a beautiful soul, Ma.

Mama, Mama, you're my lady.
You're the realest. I love you, Mama.

IF ONLY WE KNEW
A. Gab

If we only knew the two of them would be like this ... I think I would have protected them more. By that I mean, I'd have kept them locked away somewhere so they couldn't leave my sight. I never would have thought that we would lose him so soon -- and her, well, she wasn't far behind. I don't know which was worse, him dying or her trying to kill herself to be with him. The sad part is, I never saw it coming. When you have children, the last thing you tend to think of is pain and heartache. Unfortunately, there was too much of that here. I don't know if I could say where it went wrong; but what I do know is, they were attached at the hip. They would die for each other if need be. They could fight with each other, but no one could look at her funny without him puffing his chest. The same went for her with him. You would've thought her the older one, the way she protected him. So many nights we laid awake wondering where I went wrong. Why did this have to be the path they chose? As if things couldn't get worse -- I've not only lost one, but now she is gone, too ... locked away like an animal. In a way, it's probably a good thing he isn't here to see that, because I don't think he would have dealt with it too well. The one thing I always knew is that she could beat this monster, rise above the dark cloud that has hung so heavily for so long. I just know that she has the strength. She has made it through this for a reason, and I refuse to believe it was all for nothing. The one thing that they have taught me, if nothing else, is to never take life or the ones you love for granted. You never know when it'll all be gone.

THE GIRL
wi VT participant

Pretty woman — is it true what I see?
those red scars all over your arms
and bruises on your knee?

This is not a perfect body — not for
anyone to see; but let me tell you
what I know when everyone looks at me:

The girl with the lazy eye that ruins
her whole face; the one who runs so funny
she never wins a race;

the girl who gets in so many fights always
suspended from school; who skips class
and whoops ass - don't take her for a fool.

The girl who isolates and never sees
the light of day — she stays inside her house,
in the dark - on her couch is where she lay.

The girl with needle marks that cover her
from head to toe. She said she'd never
do drugs. I never thought she'd stoop so low.

The girl who's locked up in jail again, her son
with DCF - though she tries to pretend
none of this has happened.

She tries to hide the truth.
The scars all over her body
are of her tortured youth.

This body tells my story, mark for mark
some so bad you can see them in the dark.
But don't judge me. I've had enough of that.

Can't you see, without this journey
I wouldn't be me.

YOU IN 2018
   Dani

So, this is you
        target practice with a knife
to the same goals you've
        had your entire life.
Tap your heels. Go back to Oz.
You're doing the whole thing for
the wrong cause.
Do it for you.
        I like the sound of your laugh.

THEY CALLED HER KAY
Cindy

She grew up with a lazy eye.
Her mother brought her to a
'quack' as she recalls it.
She was young and really didn't know
what the outcome of going to a quack
would do.
She said, it ruined her.
All she could do was cry.
She felt ugly,
worse than before. Thinking
she'll be alone forever.
But she married when she was 30,
bore two children,
was a wonderful wife and mother.
What was extraordinary about her
was her personality, her beautiful soft skin
and when she cooked you knew
it was always delicious.
On a budget, the peasant dishes
she prepared were in today's finest cuisines,
and cost a pretty penny.
She was perfect, had a laugh
that would make you roll on the floor.
I'm so sorry she felt ugly
because she wasn't in my eyes,
she was beautiful.
My teacher, my best friend.
Exceptional in every way.
She was mine, I was hers.
She was my Mom and Moms love you
more than anyone else will ever love you.

BOOGEYMAN
M. Ga

Sat alone in the dark beneath the covers in my bed
playing over and over these words in my head.
I couldn't fall asleep, cause that Monster was alive.
Had to be alert enough so I could run and hide.
I pictured him green with fangs and batty wings
trying to drag me under by yanking dropping limbs.
I cried for my mother. I needed her help.
My friends could never know, and I would never tell.
I called this thing the Boogeyman who lingered in the dark,
even though my mom would say that monsters are a farce.
But I remember how I felt, that fear doesn't subside.
I relive it again when I go back in time.
I'm older now, I've conquered fear.
I know there's probably nothing there.
I venture to the great unknown
to face my trouble bad as bold.
I'll show them all nothing holds me back,
until I met this one guy, Z.

His face was gentle, his voice was kind;
how could I ever be so blind?
He proceeded to tell me a story about a time
he stole a Ferrari, broke into people's houses in the middle of the night,
holding them hostage with a switchblade knife …
Took all he could get and then he'd bounce somewhere off the map,
nowhere to be found. He called himself the Boogeyman,
looked at the boys in blue 'catch me if you can.'

It's funny when you take a different point of view.
And it hurts so badly when there's nothing you can do.
He must be a product of his society,
watched his mama struggle for a simple bite to eat.
Going through Christmas without the gifts
after being a good boy, drawing out his list.
Watching his friends lose their lives
in a gunfight, couldn't save theirs but risked his own to try.
That lifestyle turned that boy into a man.
He's only just surviving, and you never lent a hand.
You'll watch a person beg you on the corner of the street
standing with a cardboard sign and no shoes on his feet.
You drive right by paying very little thought,
but you'll never forget the look that you caught.
So just remember how far a good deed can go.
Help out your neighbor who's hurting and low.

GRAMPI *(Excerpt)*
  wi VT participant

The past is not always a nice place to go. Lies, the ugly home-made clothes, the coldness from the cellar's dirt floor; greasy hair, dirty face…

Grampi is home. He will take care of me, he always does. Washes my face, feeds me candy, sits me on the arm of the chair to watch TV with him. We both fall asleep in the big comfortable chair. Even though he has a big bed that is warm upstairs. He sleeps in the chair so I will know he is there.

So, when I start to remember, I try to make sure Grampi is there.

WHAT FUELS ME
Sarah

I wonder if you could ever really remove everything that provokes a fear response. Instincts are imperative to survival, singularly, and as a race. If I remove all fear, what do I become? It seems to me a path fated for doom. At the height of my own demise, I know that the fear kept me alive and I have to be thankful for that. Though, I do know there are different dimensions to this complicated feeling, with tendrils, branching out into myself. Trapping me, inside this cage, with chains of steel, and unbreakable locks, labeled kindly, *do not touch*. I would squeeze my eyes shut if I wasn't so terrified of the dark. Is it holding my eyes open, steady and unblinking, that keeps me safe? Is it the light in my eyes what keeps what is lurking at bay? The steady beat of my heart is what I grip on to. I clench my teeth and I brace for impact. It's all right here now. I will never be, everything. I must be insane because I love to feel it. I stuff it down, and I use it. It fuels me, the sustenance for my inspiration.

THE BEAUTY BENEATH
M. Ga

Nobody ever saw the beauty underneath,
didn't take the time to see her standing on those mountain peaks.
She rose above every tribulation in her life,
gave you everything she had without thinking twice.
As a child, she grew up oldest one of three;
she was the captain of her cheerleading team.
At 15 years old, she faced more than she could juggle,
every day she woke up knowing it would be a struggle.
Her mother worked three jobs at a nursing home,
left a note on the counter with a can of Spaghetti O's.
'Throw it in the microwave, get back to bed on time,
make sure to turn off the lights, I won't be back 'til five.'

Her father lived his own life separate from all that.
She called him by his first name, didn't know him as Dad.
The memories she had of him beating her down
threatened to kill her if she muttered a sound.
Her mother just watched, hopeless. What was she supposed to do?
If she tried to stop him, then she would get it too.
Came home with her ears pierced, he ripped it out of her lobe,
said she wouldn't be dressed like that living inside of his home.
Her friends couldn't see those nasty conditions.
To conceal her secret life was her daily mission.

So, you know what she did when she found herself a boy
who was four years older; he treated her like a toy.
He provided her needs and he didn't beat her
and the things he told her were a whole lot sweeter.
He showed her the escape and she saw the way out.
She moved in with him and that's when two kids came about.
She never got to go on to college or cheer teams;
so much for chasing all of those big dreams.
Now she works at her own kids
and still feels to this day she didn't do something right.
She left their father after the oldest turned two
and after the fifth time she found him breathless and blue.
And the cycle begins, a single-handed mother
raising up a family with no help from the father.
But she vowed to herself that she'd do something different
and her actions proved she wholeheartedly meant it.
Gave them both something better than what she had
and to see where they're at now she couldn't be happier.
They broke that cycle, they're both married and grown,
moved out of state; on Christmas, they fly back home.
Beautiful things born from some terrible life
those times are the past and the time is flying by.

NOTHING HAS CHANGED
Tess

Everything is the same today as it was three years ago. Everything except my body, its shape, its quickness to alert me when I'm in pain, needing rest and needing quiet space to reflect. I have a daily routine: sleep, crochet, sleep, eat little, sleep, watch TV. Sleep.

And while I'm sleeping, I dream of heroin, pot, fast cars and a crazy life. While I'm awake, I think, rethink, contemplate, think about thinking how to change my body so that it thinks slower, rewinds my thought processes. Breaking the chain of my distorted thinking. Why I dream of heroin instead of crack, I do not know. I've put a lot of thought into how my body is reacting to a lifetime of abuse, misuse and neglecting myself.

I feed an addiction so powerful, but yet I don't feed the maternal instinct to mother my two children looking at me in bright wide eyes, asking in a way as to say, *How can you become who you need to be to love me, care for me and nurture us back as a whole?* I need to starve every thought that leads me away from the person I really am deep inside. When I'm in my addiction, I need to starve the thoughts that go into doubting myself, into thinking just one more. I need to starve the party.

Lacking the ability to nurture my sons and feed the hurt away has been my demise. I am in the last year of my 30's. What will the next decade look like for me? I couldn't bear to think of it as another ten years of a blur, locked in jail, failure feeding me until I crawl up into a ball and decay surrounded by women feeding their addictions and starving success. Starving the second and third charge to become more than their mistakes.

My body is remembering the last 30 years and how it's gotten me to where I am today. Nothing has changed, but there are thoughts that try interrupting my days to wonder: *hope — has it faded out or arrived?*

WHAT IS MINE
A. Gab

I have withered to a heaping pile of skin and bones to reclaim what is rightfully mine. I sat alone and sucked the life out, my heart, my soul, while sucking the substance from the spoon. I thought that I was injecting the antidote to my pain and sorrow directly from the source, I thought that was the answer. Why come to the light when the darkness envelopes and protects my fragile mind from spinning and my frail heart from breaking … it seemed to make sense. All the while I fed my demon, it not only grew, it became all I knew. While the me I wanted was shriveling and dying, gasping for precious air, this thing no one knew was filling my skin. Seems funny that I couldn't return, but when I saw the demon, it was deceptive and stronger than I'd ever care to admit. My antidote was poison, killing everything good that resonated in my bones.

Only I could stop, only I could conquer. A skeleton has no weight in a fight with a mass such as this. I was thrown around. How long do you stay down before you get back up? Well, that's just it, I will not stay down and crumble. I will reclaim what is rightfully mine.

"I walked in a summer twilight ..."
   L. Bell

I walked in a summer twilight searching for my daughter.
Along the path, I remembered the times when we
would go on walks holding hands and laughing.
Searching for my daughter, I had to remember
she is no longer a little girl but a young lady
and the world had more meaning for her now
at this age.

It was there in the beautiful pasture surreal,
by wild flowers she sat just taking in the beauty
and fresh air.

It was then that I sat with her and placed
my arm around her, looking at the beauty
of all things. Once again another day
of happiness with my daughter and a memory
never to forget.

THE SIGNS OF CAPTURE
Louise

Captured in a facility for months, with other moms.
Captured like a monkey in a cage.
Captured by the first signs of renewal, like the flower.
Captured by a penny that I just found yesterday, face-up. Luck!
Captured by all the infinity signs I can see everywhere in one day ...
Happy!
Captured by the art class that I attend with a lot of interest . . . where I
just rest.
Captured by the monarch that I painted with watercolor just two days
after the birthday of my son . . . who followed my path.
Captured by the moon as simply a full and wonderful moon bringing in
few seconds emptiness . . . sadness!
Captured by trying to let go in my mind always ... my ex ...
Capture, capture, capture . . . let me go ...
The signs of coming back ... take the road, Jack and prepare your
backpack!

DEAR OLD JAN
Emily

There are many women in my family that I could write about. Naturally, my mother comes first to mind, for I have never known anyone who is as hard-working and loving as she. I hold her in the highest regard. There is one in my family who has been very underappreciated, well at least by me.

Dear old Jan. Jan, the sister of my grandmother who, much to my displeasure, outlived my grandmother. She was not very warm, unless she had a martini. Her sophisticated and biting wit sent at least two waitresses running for cover, from what I remember of eating out with her. There were never any children to play with at her homes. Her two well-connected marriages gave no children. I often harbored the fear that she would cook me if I didn't behave.

There are things I know about her but didn't understand when I was small; and things I only now can guess at since her passing.

I know that she was a major influence in educating incarcerated women. She was even recognized and awarded at the UN for her efforts. I know because I knocked over the picture frame and was almost cooked. She gave generously to all kinds of programs. There is even a plaque at the Music Hall with her name because of a large donation. It was placed there after my first real appearance on that stage in "South Pacific." She was there opening night.

I remember all kinds of good things from all over the world in her house. Especially the statue of the rain god from Peru, because without fail every time I rubbed its back, it rained.

I remember the Boy Scout camp next to her home that she financed to build, just to keep all the "damn boys out of the road."

Or her cashmere sweater that isn't really important at all, except that is how I remember her when I think fondly of her. Grey soft sweater, white pearls around her neck. Our last conversation, our last game of *20 Questions*.

I didn't know how to appreciate her like I do now. I always felt she hated me. Yet a bed was always waiting for my visits. Every summer camp adventure was because of her generosity. She has done so much, and now, too late, she has my awe and appreciation.

MAKING READY
   Dani

Everything seems ready
        (with nothing set in stone).
I'm a ball of nerves
        (although none of it is shown).
Let's start this out at the top of my delight.
Look how much the girls have grown.
I'll light a candle for each one of them.
One for the eldest, what a gem!
When it comes to conforming, she's the best.
Then there's M — yeah, there's beauty and smarts.
She's lacking in grace (gravity hates us).
3rd is my baby, with a precious face,
caught a spider and named him Gus.
The 4th is for me. Well, no.
We can't do that; it wouldn't glow.
4th is for painting because that's my vice.
My daddy is my hero, so I guess
we'll light another.
Maybe a shout out and one more
for my brother.
Well, I'm already to 6
and I still have no room for me.
The wax is melting into a thick molten sea.
I wonder why…
I tend to care in the wrong places,
looking for truth within lying faces.
Too many candles, no wonder it's one per day.
There's no fight for space.
This is a celebration in every spark.

WHAT HOLDS ME BACK
M. Ga

I have titled what holds me back. I have named it. I have cursed it. I have despised and hated it. It's a thief of dreamers. A thief of hope. It does not play fair, and always kept me on my toes. But I stood up for myself one day. I thought to myself, *no guts, no glory*. I went all in. I let go of what was grounding me, bridling me. Had me like a puppet on a string. And just like that, it was all in my control to let something go that had so much power like that. But I did it. The battle didn't end there. It haunted me like a ghost. It snuck up on me when I least expected, inviting me back for one more taste. I hesitate. I start to believe the lie. Maybe it's not so bad. Maybe it will be different. But come on, we've been through this before. We know how it ends. The void it leaves will never be filled. Yet the emptiness is better than having a monkey on your back.

QUESTIONS FOR THE INSIDE
A. Gab

So many times, I've learned that the most important, meaningful conversations are held with self. The mind wanders where no spoken words can go. All truths are freed, there are no boundaries. I have contemplated so many master plans, sophisticated and fool proof. In my mind, I had all the answers and I was always right. Lover or enemy, the space you potentially rented was vast. It's all or nothing, even in the crazy mixed up thoughts of my head. Thoughts have consumed and sickened my soul when I didn't want them to … but there is nowhere to hide. Why is it that switch cannot be flipped?

I've tried to figure the answer out, to no avail. It stays the same. I've heard the phrase, *you are only as sick as your secrets,* many times; and truth be told, it resonates a little too much. Secrets have held a grip on my heart in ways that no chains could bear. No lover has spun the web strong enough to free these things I keep so tightly sealed, no enemy strong enough to bring forth the darkest parts I have inside. If there was a way to put it all out there, I have to say that I wouldn't … that is the one thing that can't be taken from me, the one thing I don't have to share.

ADHD

wiVT participant

Ima let my mind wander today. In school, I had to sit still and behave. From 4th to 6th grade my Mom sprinkled Adderall in my cereal. She didn't tell my teachers or me, because she didn't want my teachers to treat me differently. I learned some skills on how to focus, like turning the ticking clock into white noise.

My mom one time was at a restaurant in France back when she did a backpacking trip through Europe. The waiter asked her if she wanted more. Instead of saying, "No, I'm full," she said that she was pregnant.

I've had many blonde moments in my life. One being that it was dark out and I ran into the screen door. That's not the worst part. I tried two more times to walk through it. Yes, I was sober.

People have called me stupid, dumb, blonde, whore, bitch. Told me, I was rude, and did that instigating shit with me. I may have made some bad decisions, but I'm not stupid. Being anywhere on the autism spectrum, we are all truly incredible. Our senses are super heightened and we notice things that others don't. So next time you wanna make fun of somebody like that, just know that they could be smarter than you are.

I'm unique. I'm proud.

If people don't like me they're S.O.L. There are 7 billion people in this world. Love me or hate me, but you're still thinking of me. I'm okay with myself. No one is here in my life forever. They're either going to drift away or die. Ima rebel for life. Find me where the wild things are. If I like you, I won't forget about you. Don't you worry.

"I know I need to belong to myself" (*excerpt*)
    Tess

I have a hunger in my belly, a fire in my eye and the world's my apple. I can split it up as I choose. Apple pie, apple cobbler or just a plain shiny Granny Smith, spit shined by the bottom of my t-shirt, to eat whenever I'm ready, however I choose.

I simply hate letting fear drive me into choices where I become the shadow of someone else. I need to unhate the thing I so comfortably knew and grew to love. I unloved myself.

I unloved the freedom of Tess. And everything about Tess. Whatever I belong to, I want to become.

JEALOUSY

wiVT participant

When you least expect it, Jealousy can blow in like an ill wind and swirl and twist until it feels a form. Tall and lanky with an attractive red cap and green skin - naturally - and a smile not unlike a Cheshire Cat.

A shape-shifter, Jealousy can be your best friend or worst enemy. His shiny black cape can turn a sunny day dark when placed just the right way. His matching black briefcase can swallow joy and accomplishment, pride and hope when the lock opens and a few hasty words escape. If you see Jealousy approach, beware. He is not your friend.

Life Lines

LETTERS HOME TO MOM
Tess

Mom,
Could you please pay my bills while I'm away? Rent's due in June. M
says he owes $220.00 on the lights. The cats are low on food and Z
needs clothes. The car needs to be registered and insurance is due in
July. I've added you to the policy. I can only afford liability. I'm giving
you extra money for your tires for your van. Please park my car in town.
The tires need to be changed. Make sure when you change the oil, have
them calibrate my car right to the odometer. Please make sure to pay the
$70.00 parking ticket. My car is at risk of being towed while you go into
town. That would be a run of bad luck. See you in July. Hope there's
enough left for you to go play the slots or bingo. Love you and thanks for
picking up the slack.

***

I keep shouting. You stand gripping the phone as my voice gets louder.
Where are you? Can you hear me? I'm trying to pull at the love that
hangs in the air, give reason to stay, please. You're blinking really fast. I
can picture you staring blankly at the wall, trying to put all of it
together. Our finances are at the center of our lives, ripping us apart.
Can you please tell me what you're thinking? You can go speechless as
my emotions turn to a frantic pitch. I go numb. I'm out of breath.
You've lost the fight. I'm already halfway out of the door and I've yet to
come home. The bills continue to drain my pockets. There's food on the
table. The roof's not leaking. Isn't that enough…wouldn't you say?

***

I received your Mother's Day card today. I wanted to thank you for thinking of me. I'm honored to be called "Mom" by you. You are exceptional because between my wrongs and God's rights, he made you perfectly. I am blessed to have you. I want you to know I love you and I'm really excited to have you in my life today. I hope your heart's lighter after all those years. I promise next year we will be together on my special day.

***

You forgot to pay my parking ticket. Such is luck, I guess you went to bingo instead. Hope you are luckier than me. Please pay it. The car might get towed if you go into town. Such would be your luck.

Love,
Your Daughter

MY PURE SPACE
Jayden

HE - is a pure space.
A slow night passes and my heart knocks
like a thunderstorm at sea.

A simple minute passes.
And everything changes.
He is a complete instrument,
he is happiness waiting to unravel with me.

He is a vine waiting to grow,
waiting to flower and bloom
creating light and beauty wherever he goes.

He is a song waiting to be sung
by love doves born in a solitary burst.

He is my pure space.

MY BIRTHDAY IN PRISON

wiVT participant

Today is January 21st, 2016 and it's my birthday. Having my birthday celebrated here was an amazing experience, because all of my friends in House 1 made it an amazing day. They made me a beautiful birthday card and gave me a very funny gift. A few of the girls in House 1 made me laugh so hard that my face turned red. My dear friend Cindy gave me some coffee for my birthday, which I thought was very sweet of her. My other birthday gift was when I went down to see my caseworker and she told me that she put my resident check through to my probation officer and that I will be going home this coming week. The rest of my day went by as normal. Then it was time to go to writing class. When I get back to the unit, I plan on playing cards with my cell mate. That is how I spent my birthday in prison. Today I feel very bubbly.

NOTES AT HOME
Cindy

Hi Honey,
I made some lasagna.
Just heat in the oven.
325° is what you put it at.
Be careful, it will be hot.
Oh yeah, there's red wine on the rack.
Enjoy!
Love,
Me

***

Hey, Nick.
It's been so long since we talked.
I miss you and the kids.
Can't wait 'til our birthday
when we'll be all together again.
Drive slow and buckle up!
And I will make your favorite dessert –
Death by Chocolate!
P. S. Call if you need anything.
Love,
Mom

***

Dear Mom and Dad,
I hope you are both fine.
Tell Albert to pick you up.
Stop whenever you need to
It's a four-hour ride
but it will be worth it.
Can't wait to see you both.
Love,
Cindy

***

Hi, Albert
You are going to pick up Mom and Dad.
Drive carefully, not fast like usual!
Are Andres and Anthony coming,
and Jamie, too?
It will be our first family sleepover
in my new house.
Love,
Cynthia

***

Dear Kevin and Tina,
I would like you to come over.
May 31st is Nick's birthday.
We are having steaks on the grill,
Filet Mignon and your favorite, Kevin,
my famous stuffed mushrooms; and, Tina

your favorite, too: Sangria.
P.S. Thanks for helping me with my new
lawn mower.
You are the best neighbors.
I appreciate all you both do
for me, all the time.
Love you guys,
Cindy

***

George,
Just wanted to say hello.
The weather has been great.
We'll have to go to the beach one day
when you have a day off.
See ya,
Cindy
P.S. I love my new pink tablet! Thx again.

***

Lorraine,
I really don't have anything to say to you.
You were so rude to my friends.
I know we have known each other
for quite a long time,
but I cannot tolerate your negativity.
I think it's best if we go our own ways.
Cindy

AND STILL WE HOPE

WHAT I SEE

wi VT participant

What did I see to be except myself?
The question still lingers in my mind.
Why try to be anything but yourself?
The answers flash away like a second in time.
All the wrong things done.
All the rough paths traveled.
None of it was me.
This I later came to see
like a mask I woke up to everyday.
Staring me back in the mirror.
I had no idea who I was looking at.
But it was really me all along.
The person I let you make me.
The person surrendered to.
I no longer let you control me.
I realize now I was who *you* wanted me to be.
Now I'm who I want to be,
never to surrender again.

IT'S NOT I, IT'S ME
Dani

I stand there, staring at my enemy.
Everywhere I look, she's there.
The first time she tried to kill me,
she cut me with a knife.
I knew what she was going to do.
I practically helped her plan it
but we recovered.
When I became a mother I saw her less and less.
Once in a while, she'd creep in,
Desperate Housewives style.
I'd get that fix that only she could offer.

The second time,
I woke up in the hospital.
She'd left me dead on the couch.
I ran right back. She'd been
the only friend I had. The only one
I deserved. We were homeless junkies
and frankly alone. She was there
to keep me warm. She was there to cheer me up.

She, SHE, for the 3rd time tried to kill me,
shaking, quivering on a kitchen floor,
wrappers of Narcan surrounding me.
The next morning, I was arrested.
I left her at the gate with my past.

Danielle was her name,
self-sabotage her game.
Every time I see old pictures,
it's not me, it's her.
Every scar, every dose. It's her.
Every bad memory. Every burned bridge.
I've worked too hard to let her try again.
I hit the mirror. It shatters.
I'll only kill her once.

GODDESSES AND HEROES
*wi*VT participant

I am sitting and writing at a table of goddesses and heroes, pondering the little I know of their situation in this labyrinth of life, and law and limits. Courage becomes an aura around each one – the hero must find and use the legendary keys – love. Love yourself, and face fears about whatever; and love even more; and remember the love, remember you and the dreams of you that you have loved; and love some more.

You are the goddess, you are the poet who has written your poems, your story; and you are your hero-self, free at last of riptides and yanking currents, free of the seaweeds that tried to grab your legs and pull you under. Your love of you is your champion and conquers the memories that make you fear or hold you back. Your love of you grows you into goddess-size and you begin to remember the good, the true, the quiet, the beautiful; and the love opens, because it is too much for just one and spills out into the ocean – an oil spill of love that does smooth the waters and carry you safely back to the shore, to the you of love and truth and beauty and maybe even peace in the sand.

At night on the beach in the summer air that feels like the safest blanket in forever, is the soft lights of full moons and millions of stars reflecting on rolling, ever moving water. This is the perfect place to be with the universe at peace. It is always there – always available from memory – peace always.

WOUNDS
Melissa

What wounds do I deny
when I admit them all?
I with stone face, shrug,
admitting unimaginable horror.
Each scar forged me harder,
stern, implacable, distant.
These wounds I admit, then,
are the source of my power.
The empathic intuition of
the hunted child
breathes character from caricature.
The billion strands of necessary
utter attention to stay alive
weave worlds on warp and weft.
The spine of steel,
unbroken and you won't break me
all determination in the face of defeat.
These wounds, my armor, my power.
These wounds, meant to rend and kill.
These wounds, necessary hardening.
These wounds I display, my power.

GETTING OUT OF TROUBLE
wiVT participant

My husband giving me drugs, getting lost in the rhythm of dealers, dealing, doing cocaine. Losing the valuable time with my family. Now in here, my life for the first time being in jail. Not being there for my first grandchild's birth. One thing leading into another. Now I'm clean, I've cried because of my loss of time. I've cried as the fog lifts. I still can't remember all the past.

I do remember some important and laughable times. Like when I made my daughter her 19th birthday cake with the last of the miniature statues that went along with a graveyard cake. A red velvet cake with another whole bottle of red food coloring added to it. It came out dark blood red. I added candy skulls and crossbones to the batter. Topping was chocolate pudding with crushed Oreos for dirt. Milano cookies put into the top with an edible pen writing each name of every person in the house as headstones. Gummy bears, heads chopped off. A large plastic spider on top center. Gummy worms everywhere. The story goes: we are dead, dead, the ground flowing with all of our blood. Come to the laboratory to see where it all happened!

I remember the fun of calling my daughter and her boyfriend back home. To be spookier still all I did when she answered, was a loud and as terrifying a scream as I could muster. I hung up quickly. I got a text, *What was that!!!???* My return text was *Come and see where it all happened*. We all laughed and enjoyed this super moist interesting cake and story line. My regret was a month before, selling my camera to get more drugs. All these years later we still laugh remembering my daughter's 19th birthday. She adores Halloween, her birthday is October 29th.

Now clean and sober, my children and I wait for my husband to come home. I have a fresh start with grandchildren. So being swept away, away from those I love and love me in return. The tides have turned.

CREATION
wiVT participant

Move, move, walk through
emotions, no judgment
set it, feel it, it's a part of you
yet doesn't define you

whittle, whittle, shaving wood
revealing what you are ready to see
carving some secrets still

turning, peeling, giving, growing
keep the knife sharp for a clean cut
moving into yourself, moving out of yourself,

seeing who you are and who you are not
joy, fear, wood, metal, all working together
as one, creating a masterpiece that is you

Keep the knife sharp and a clean cut
know what you want for you and go for it.
Discover who you are.

HOW DO YOU GET TO THE POINT?
wiVT participant

I have had many disappointments and heartaches in life. They've come from family, friends, acquaintances, and some who have just crossed my path. I've also had many joys in life, coming from the same sources. I do let myself get excited, joyous and happy about something I'm passionate about.

But I don't let myself get bothered by negativity. I don't believe in fighting or yelling; nor do I take part in name-calling or anything of the sort. I am very optimistic and see the good in everyone. I believe everyone has the potential to do and be good – even though we all have our faults.

How do you get to the point of not letting stuff bother you? I wasn't always like this.

It takes practice. I don't hold resentments. I give everyone second chances, being more patient with people. I've learned to let things roll. We are all human, after all. I live my life to the full extent. Every path I've chosen has made me the person I am today.

THE BRIDGE
Melissa

A bridge between starshine and clay
perceivably fragile, gossamer moonbeams.
Buffeted by roaring sea,
salt formed clay, sturdier than expected.
Battered by the builder,
a thousand times, a mystery,
leaves nary an outward mark.
Slashed by beastly claws,
perpetual knocking down a peg,
lest a span across responsibility
get "uppity."
Withered by scorn no more
Solidified, Triumphant,
Starshine stronger than steel.

PIECE OF ME
wiVT participant

Suddenly and everywhere,
there stood a piece of me,
with parts unknown and parts misunderstood.
It set my mind at ease.
As the brush glides and my thoughts flow,
it felt like a river in Egypt.
My emotions and feelings grew
as if I were telling my life story.
With so much to say and so little time,
I had to squeeze it all in.
As I turn to my right with respect and grace,
and a smile coming from within,
I proudly say: *This is me, strong and different.*
Suddenly and everywhere,
there stood a piece of me!

SCENE OF JOY
Emily

Flour is spilled across the floor leaving it fully coated. It is as if snow has fallen inside, dusted thickly, heaping in drifts. A part of me could almost consider lying down and attempting a snow angel. But there is a suspicious glob of egg yolk I'd rather avoid. If the floor is a snowstorm, then the counter is a hurricane. Spices add splashes of color to the white flour. Egg and milk can be found in abundance. Thick gooey globs are everywhere and continue to pile beneath the little hands at the heart of the mess. She stands there in her too-large apron grinning from ear to ear. Hands that look like they belong to a master sculptor up to their elbows in plaster.

Today is our baking day. My favorite day. I am in love with the smells that remind me of my grandmother. I remember rising early to go and find her preparing the breads, sweet rolls, and pies. Normally a ghost to the kitchen, it was fascinating to watch her and to eventually learn from her.

The tradition continues as my little padawon joins me. We have *Hairspray* in the CD player. We are laughing, we are messy, and wow!, are we joyous.

These are the days, the moments, with my kitchen a mess that I would not trade for anything, or change the one beside me.

BURN OF MEMORY (excerpt)
A. Gab

Set the flame to those sleepless nights,
and watch them dissipate into the air.
Torch the insecurities that scream my name
with venom. I have the antidote now that
sucks the poison from the words.
Stir the ashes, stoke the fire, feed it with
more gasoline.

Scald those memories, painted black with
sheets of tears.
They turn to dust and I toss them
in the wind.
Throw into the fire the addiction that had
me by the throat.
I breathe so much easier these days, now
that the constriction is cut loose.

I know I'm a
little more free than I was yesterday.
I'll watch the flames turn to embers,
then to ashes, keeping just enough
to remember.

PAINTING YOUR LIFE
Dani

My world began in white and black.
Not black and white like you'd typically expect.
Most of the white was slowly changing
to gray the older I got until one day I got a cut,
and a deep burgundy dripped from my veins.
Whenever I craved to see color, I knew
where to turn. A nick here and a razor blade there,
until black was the color that ran out of me.

The next color was a small blue line
and when I snorted it, the sky was blue;
and a green pill crushed up and ingested made me
see green grass. I'd cracked the code.
I'd finally found a way to live without all the blacks
and greys, but it always ran out. You always have
to start over. The more I did, the brighter life became;
but the darker my picture was when my powdery paint
was gone, Until one day there was no color.
I tried and tried but the color never came.
I put the paint right to my veins and a dim glow came
to the distance. *More,* I thought; and more is what I did.

White was all I saw and when I woke up,
straight to black. You think you've got it
all figured out. When you start with one color,
it makes light; but the more you add, the darker
you'll get. You can't make yellow with black and grey,
and you can't make blue with all of your pain at the end
of the day. When your canvas is white, start slow
and you'll make it right. Your attitude is like a pallet
of colors constantly painting your life.

LIFE LINES

"Something has tried to kill me and has failed" -Lucille Clifton
   A Gab

A fight to the death, to the end of limits, knocked down and bruised, but begging for more of the toxicity within. You have dragged me by the weakest of limbs through depths of hell that are unheard of. A slave of sorts, I fall to my knees, right on the highway of self-medicating. How many times have you brought me to the brink of death? It's a never-ending carousel, spinning me into a pathetic web of lies.

Bury me in the very little pills that I seek for comfort. If I'm going to die anyway, suffocate me with oblivion and as many CC's of that magical potion as my veins will hold. A system overload of darkness knocking in my head, telling me to give in. A whole life wasted, a means of escape and I've sinned again. I really don't want to say that this is my comfort, but the truth hurts and I can't deny it anymore.

I want to seek the light, really I do. I want to love life through the crystal- clear vision I was once given. I have tried to survive and somehow still stand. How do I trust something with such force that has taken so much from me? I've watched and prayed for better days since I can remember. It seems like our time has been interrupted, merely arrested.

Will it be a life sentence, or the death penalty? The devil, the judge, and his minions, the jury – the darkness is real but it won't keep me hostage.

MANIC
Sarah

On a piece of spontaneity with every emotion flooding me to the brim, I can't swim out and I can't reach the edge. I swirl through a rotary around and around, allowing myself a piece in this puzzle I've left unmastered, left unfinished with many hands holding the pieces. We are never finished.

Where we started, this vast emptiness, splattered only with the blackness we allow, what takes form to the shapes that we create. It is us. It's a life force; crack it open and you can see it pulsing. It is not an illusion. What we have created we can master; we have handed out the pieces and we can make them fit.

What was once can be again, what has always been will always be, and what was never meant to happen will never come to pass. We can't will things into existence. We can just be.

"an instrument in the shape of a woman ..."
    L. Bell

I am an instrument in the shape of a woman.
Graceful, angelic, strong, bold
making music, enjoying every note.

I am an instrument in the shape of a woman.
Loud with strength
blasting through the crowd drawing attention
to my melody and structure.

I am an instrument in the shape of a woman.
Drum, flute, violin, electric guitar, horn, it's anyone's guess.
How is my mood? Guess.
Where am I?
How am I feeling?
Where have I gone or been?

I feel like I am an instrument in the shape of a woman.

THE HAPPY FLU
Cindy

It must be because
spring is in the air.
But lately, after lock in
my room, the four of us, we laugh and laugh.
We got so loud
last night the next room
told us to shut up.
Everything we said was hilarious.
Our cheeks were hurting,
our faces were beet-red,
it took all I had in me
not to pee my pants.

I haven't laughed that much
in such a long time.
What we were laughing about
I cannot tell you.
But, it has been the third night in a row.
We laughed like laughing fools
and the subject hasn't changed.
I can't wait for tonight,
I hope it happens again.
Laughter in jail, the medicine
you can take.
It doesn't come in a pill.
We laughed like we were kids again.

MY DEAR CHILDREN
Valerie

Safety doesn't mean not letting people in. Security doesn't mean money alone. Freedom doesn't mean only doing what you want and happiness doesn't mean getting your way all the time. You have each other and that's my gift to you. The time will come when friends will come and friends will go. The day will come when "he" will break your heart or when he'll make your day. And the one person who will be there for you, through hell or high water and come what may, is your sister. Help each other through thick and thin. I'll be here for as long as I can, as Nana was for me. But time still passes and the seasons of life still stroll. One day I will go to sleep, like Nana did for me. Be there always for one another. Stand behind the other, strong and loud and proud. And know that I'm always proud of you, on Earth or from a cloud.

THE FOUNDATION ON WHICH WE BUILD
Sarah

Speaking things into existence. Essentially creating something from nothing. Words have power. And that power is gripping me like a vice. I have a constant urge to do something large, make an impact. I wonder how I can make my voice the hammer that breaks the glass of the box that is holding us inside?

If I am a queen, then I should treat myself as royalty, and others as well. That would make an impact. Others might not understand it, but they would feel it. It would stir something in them to find answers, to gain knowledge. Imagine how perplexed you would be to have a stranger treat you as though you were made of gold. I like to think it would drive most to kindness. If that happens, words will have created it.

They are the foundation on which we build. We need only grasp the endless possibilities. Why is it we see anything as unobtainable? I can't just be a hopeless optimist. There must be passion in the hearts of the masses. We need to be fearless. And being fearless doesn't mean not being afraid. It means that you were afraid, but did it.

AM I THIS MYSTERY WOMAN?

Who are you, holding the lifeline
letting me fade into the background
adrift in the fractals
disguising the ugliest aspects of human nature?

Poised with grace
and completely unveiled,
the daughter in the trees
waves goodbye,
thoughts escaping her like roots of a tree.

She is not one for despair;
her heart doesn't stop,
her branches spreading like wings
tangling past and present.
So much can be seen through her eyes
mixing and melding emotions
inside the mind of a dream.

Re-formed from the ash of former fire
-- flames that burn, knock you down --
she sees red,
yelling into the darkness
STOP! to past choices or demons in her head.

She deals with relentless want;
no joy is born without its sorrow.
All I really see is a strong woman
who believes in who she is now.

[found poem by Sarah W. Bartlett, 2.4.16]

DID YOU KNOW ...

Only four percent of the world's female population lives in the United States — yet the United States accounts for over thirty percent of the world's incarcerated women.[1]

Research shows that female criminality is produced and sustained by: histories of personal abuse; mental illness tied to early life experiences; substance abuse and addiction; economic and social marginality; homelessness; and relationships.[2]

In Vermont, 78% of the women who are incarcerated are serving sentences for offenses that are non-violent in nature. The majority of these women are incarcerated due to substance abuse.[3]

80% of Vermont's incarcerated women have children.[4]

For women, recovery and healing is a process of transformational change that occurs in deep connection with self and others.[5]

Women-only groups have been shown to help members explore new possibilities for feeling, perceiving and behaving.[6]

Financially speaking, it would cost Vermont the same to treat addiction outside of jail as it does to incarcerate.[7]

---

[1] Kajstura, Aleks. States of Women's Incarceration: The Global Context 2018. https://www.prisonpolicy.org/global/women/2018.html.
[2] Bloom, Barbara and Stephanie Covington. Addressing the Mental Health Needs of Women Offenders, 2008.
[3] State of Vermont Governor's Commission on Prison Overcrowding, 2004.
[4] Ibid.
[5] Bloom, Barbara and Stephanie Covington. Addressing the Mental Health Needs of Women Offenders, 2008.
[6]Ibid.
[7] State of Vermont Governor's Commission on Prison Overcrowding, 2004.

DISCUSSION GUIDE

Incarcerated women are much more than statistics. They are our mothers, grandmothers, sisters, and daughters. They are our neighbors and co-workers. When an individual is seen as greater than their mistake, and inspired to contribute to a larger entity by example and participation, personal transformation can begin. *Choose one piece of writing from this collection that resonates with you. If you could speak with the author of the piece, what would you want to say to her in the context of this bigger picture?*

Research suggests that trauma victims require social support to recover and heal, because trauma always occurs within a social context and 'social wounds require social healing.'[8] *writinginsideVT* sessions contribute to a shared mission of rehabilitation and restorative justice by helping to repair the harms caused by an offender's actions while also rebuilding community and relationships. *As family members and neighbors of incarcerated women, how can we be lifelines for them within our communities?*

It is often said that when we incarcerate a woman we incarcerate her family. Many collateral consequences remain after a sentence is served, which makes successful re-entry difficult. *What do you think is the most overlooked collateral consequence? What systemic approach(es) can we take to minimize all such consequences?*

As you read the words of these writers, *where did you find connection and where did you find disconnection? Which sentiment was stronger? What can you learn from this?*

One definition of 'lifeline' is 'a means of communication for receiving or delivering assistance.' *In what ways do you feel a program such as writinginsideVT provides a lifeline for the incarcerated?*

---

[8]Covington, Stephanie. *The Relational Theory of Women's Psychological Development: Implications for the Criminal Justice System.* Female Offenders: Critical Perspectives and Effective Interventions, 2nd Edition, 2007.

ABOUT *WRITINGINSIDEVT*
WRITINGINSIDEVT.COM

PRESS and PUBLICATIONS

'writing inside VT Fall Read-Around' by Coralee Holm, City of South Burlington, Vermont blog, November 18, 2016

'Justice Center Announces Writing Program,' under Municipal Matters, *The Other Paper of South Burlington*, VT, page 9. October 27, 2016

'I Am Who I Was and So Much More,' by Sarah W. Bartlett, in *Chrysalis: The Journal of Transformative Language Arts*, September 2015

'Book Review—Hear me, see me: Incarcerated women write,' by Cassadi Marino, in *Affilia: Journal of Women and Social Work*, volume 30, issue 2, pp 271-2, Sage Publications, May 1, 2015

Author's Note on "Hear Me, See Me," by Sarah W. Bartlett in *The Mom Egg*, January 2015

Angie, one of our writers, was interviewed on 10-8-14 on WDEV radio's 'The Vermont Conversation,' featuring Vermont's hidden voices.

RETN video of "Hear Me, See Me" reading at Burlington Book Festival, September 2014

'Top 10 Picks for the 10th Annual Burlington Book Festival,' *Burlington Free Press*, September 14, 2014

'Incarcerated women subject of book, summit,' *Burlington Free Press* Staff, September 10, 2014

'History Written as Beauty: Incarcerated Women Write' by Sarah W. Bartlett, *Wellesley College Review of Books*, April 2014

LIFE LINES

'Soulful Connections Spring from Prison Writing Program' by Marybeth Redmond, *National Catholic Reporter,* December 3, 2013

'Going to jail has given me a whole new life,' about writer Raven Peres by Abby Bliss, *Brattleboro Reformer*, November 9, 2013

'Vermont Women Inmates heal through writing circle; publish book of their prose and poetry,' *Associated Press,* November 3, 2013 via *FoxNews*

'VT Women Inmates Find Outlet in Writing,' by Lisa Rathke, Associated Press

'Incarcerated Women Pen Their Stories,' Molly Walsh interviews Marybeth Redmond, WCAX-TV (CBS Affiliate, Burlington, VT)

"Hear Me, See Me: Incarcerated Women Write," ed. Marybeth Redmond and Sarah W. Bartlett, Orbis Books, 2013

Vermont Edition: 'The Poetry & Prose of Women Behind Bars, 'Jane Lindholm interviews Sarah W. Bartlett, Vermont Public Radio, October 2, 2013

Idyll Banter: 'Seeing – and Hearing – That Voice Behind Bars,' by Chris Bohjalian, *Burlington Free Press*, September 29, 2013

'One Dignified Moment' by Marybeth Redmond, *Vermont Public Radio* Brunch, January 1, 2013

'Heart of Art: Writing from the Inside Out," by Maddie McGarvey, *Burlington Free Press*, November 11, 2012

PUBLIC SPEAKING and READINGS

'writing inside VT: Writing for Change', a panel presentation with Sarah . Bartlett and Meg Reynolds at Gemini Ink Writers Second Annual Conference, San Antonio, Texas, July 2017

'Story-Telling in Non-Traditional Settings: Writing inside Prison,' Sarah W. Bartlett, keynote talk, Pennsylvania Conference of Teachers of English and Language Arts, October 2016

'Writing to Heal: Creating Safe Circles Inside Prison,' Sarah W. Bartlett, keynote talk, League of Vermont Writers Annual Meeting, January 2016

"Hear Me, See Me" author readings: Burlington, VT Book Festival, 9/14; Middlebury College, 4/14; Burlington, VT Book Launch, 10/13

"Hear Me, See Me: Incarcerated Women Write," Sarah W. Bartlett presenting the newly-launched book at the Juvenile Justice Conference in Portland, ME. October 2013

ABOUT WOMEN WRITING for (a) CHANGE, the foundational work upon which *writinginsideVT* is based:

'Youth, Writing and Identity: An Interview with Sarah W. Bartlett' by Ruth Farmer in "Transformative Language Arts in Action," ed. Ruth Farmer and Caryn Mirriam-Goldberg; R&L Education, December 2014

'Women Writing for (a) Change: History, Philosophy, Programs,' by Sarah W. Bartlett in "Women on Poetry: Writing, Publishing and Teaching," ed. Carol Smallwood, Colleen S. Harris and Cynthia Brackett-Vincent. Jefferson, NC: McFarland & Company, Inc., 2012

'Women Writing for (a) Change: Mirror, Model, Mentor' by Sarah W. Bartlett, in "Contemporary American Women: Our Defining Passages," Carol Smallwood and Cynthia Brackett-Vincent. Maine, *All Things That Matter Press,* December 2009

"Women Writing for (a) Change: A Guide for Creative Transformation, "by Mary Pierce Brosmer, *Sorin Books*, Notre Dame, IN. 2009. [Mary Pierce Brosmer is the 1991 founder of *Women Writing for (a) Change,* a national women's writing community of which Sarah W. Bartlett is the licensed Vermont affiliate.]

LIFE LINES EDITORIAL TEAM

Bianca Viñas

Bianca is an MFA candidate in the Writing & Publishing Program at Vermont College of Fine Arts. She has been working with *writinginsideVT* and this anthology since moving to Vermont two years ago. Bianca is currently completing her first novel, a hybrid work of poetry, medical research and narrative prose.

Sarah W. Bartlett, M.A., D.Sc.

Sarah's work has appeared in *Adanna, Ars Medica*, the *Aurorean, Chrysalis, Minerva Rising, Mom Egg Review, PoemMemoirStory, Women's Review of Books*; anthologies including the award-winning "Women on Poetry," McFarland & Co. Inc., 2012; and two poetry chapbooks (Finishing Line Press 2011 and 2017). Her work celebrates nature's healing wisdom and the human spirit's landscapes. She is founding co-director of *writinginsideVT* to encourage personal and social change through a supportive community within Vermont's sole women's prison.

Kassie Tibbott, Esq.

Kassie's work is dedicated to empowering others through education and community building. Kassie started volunteering with incarcerated women in 2016, as a part of the SPEAK Debate Prison Initiative. Later she joined *writinginsideVT* and hosted discussion groups and voter registration drives at other correctional facilities. She believes that in order to reduce recidivism it's important to help individuals find their own voice, rather than speak for them. This is where her passion and the production of this book intersect. Kassie is Coordinator of the Community Legal Information Center (CLIC), the State of Vermont's public law library located in South Royalton.

Meg Reynolds, M.A., M.F.A.

Meg is a poet, artist, and teacher living in Burlington, VT. Her work has appeared *The Missing Slate, Mid-American Review, Fugue, Utterance, Inverted Syntax,* and the anthology "Monster Verse: Poems Human and Inhuman" as well as "The Book of Donuts" and "With You: Withdrawn Poems of the #MeToo Movement." She is long-time facilitator and co-director of *writinginsideVT.*